To Jim Evans _ Oct. '75 —
Winner Social Science golf
tournament _ this book, for
a person who enjoys seeking
the meaning and value of
life.

A Friend & Collegue,

Monte McLaws

Eternal Man

Eternal Man

by

TRUMAN G. MADSEN

Professor of Philosophy and Religion,
Brigham Young University

and

Director of the Institute of Mormon Studies

Published by
DESERET BOOK COMPANY
Salt Lake City, Utah

1970

Library of Congress No.: 66-26092

Copyright 1966

by

DESERET BOOK COMPANY

Lithographed in U.S.A.
by
Wheelwright Lithographing Co.

Sometimes during solitude I hear truth spoken with clarity and freshness; uncolored and untranslated it speaks from within myself in a language original but inarticulate, heard only with the soul, and I realize I brought it with me, was never taught it nor can I efficiently teach it to another.

PRESIDENT HUGH B. BROWN

Introduction

In June, 1963 the first article of a memorable series was published in *The Instructor* magazine. As editors we were deeply concerned that our college-student readers might find orientation to basic philosophical problems through the insight of a scholar who knows the gospel as well as philosophy. We invited Truman G. Madsen who holds his doctorate from Harvard University and who was serving as president of the New England Mission to fill the role of author. Our first thought was a single article. Dr. Madsen submitted what is the first chapter of this book, entitled, "Whence Cometh Man???" Footnotes were not included, but they were made available by special request. Reader interest was intense and requests outstripped our limited supply. We then invited Brother Madsen to contribute six subsequent articles, one on each basic question raised in the original statement. We published complete notes for these in the magazine and received many letters from readers expressing appreciation.

The Instructor is pleased to encourage this reprint in book form for the same reasons that it published the original articles. Those reasons were set forth in the introduction which is reproduced here as follows:

President Truman G. Madsen writes both in the language of the churchman and of the philosopher. Some readers may prefer that the two viewpoints be kept separate; others may feel that the questions are beyond our adequate consideration. We grant that space is limited and that these "imponderables" have provoked volumes of argument. Yet, many serious students are reading widely today and are meeting the ideas of serious thinkers from antiquity to the present. They ask their Church leaders, "How do the arguments and positions of the various 'schools' of thought compare with the teachings of Joseph Smith and of the Restored Gospel?"

Brother Madsen answers this question, at least in part; and he does so with considerable penetration. He brings to this assignment a thorough scholarship of Church doctrine, plus an erudite schooling in philosophy, plus a deep inner conviction regarding the truthfulness of the Gospel of Jesus Christ. From this vantage point he directs the reader's attention to six basic "puzzles in philosophy and theology." He invites thinking and further study of these questions, and he challenges those whose reading may have missed the import of what some call "the long conversation." Leaders of youth need to know the ideas and language which their students meet in secular education. They need to study the arguments on basic philosophical issues. They need to understand the Gospel so that they can interpret it to these students and help them see things "of good report" in perspective.

It is to assist this serious study that we present this [introductory] article — one which we consider a notable milestone in our 97 years of publishing *The Instructor*.

LORIN F. WHEELWRIGHT
Associate Editor of *The Instructor*,
Published by the
Deseret Sunday School Union Board

Preface

The story behind these essays is still a matter of wonder in me. To a topic and title — "Whence Cometh Man???" — *The Instructor* editors added a hope. "It has been suggested," their letter said, "that you explain the meaning of premortality for some of the ultimate issues of human existence." Their intent was that I sketch in outline form the singular Mormon theme of pre-existence on the canvas of present-day philosophical approaches to man. So the effort was made.

The response was, to me at least, quite unforeseen. Not just teachers, whom we had expected to nudge toward wider application of their topics, but a variety of persons wrote for sources and further comparisons. Soon the editors asked that this article be the introduction to six others, around the issues barely broached within it: personal identity, creation, embodiment, freedom, suffering, and self-awareness. The query followed: "Will these be published in book form?" Till now I have answered, "No," convinced that interest would diminish. Instead it has increased.

Here, then, is the series, written as a kind of "midrash," a commentary on a theme. It can justly be said that they are not more than this, but not, I hope, that they are less. Letters of praise for their "objectivity" (which usually means that I have named and highlighted some of the live alternatives) miss my feeling that such merit as they have is in their subjectivity. Their primary gesture is toward inner echoes, toward, as it were, the nerve-endings of the spirit. For this reason, likewise, I am surprised at comments which assume I have proved or refuted this or that. The goal has been to clarify rather than to verify, with little room for argument, except an implicit appeal to introspection.

The concept of eternal man, with its refinements in the prophets of this new era, has an immense philosophical and theological strength which is only beginning to be recognized. But this, when presented adequately, will sponsor a tome which is not pressed for abbreviation.

It has been said more than once that the essays are hard to understand. If this reflects a struggle with the terms and the heavily packed style, my own children prove that these yield to repeated exposure. But another anxiety is involved here. Those who believe, as I do, in the magnificence of simplicity and the hazards of speculation wonder whether the statement of contrasts should be reduced or simply avoided.

Now it goes without saying that though the master writings of the Prophet are authoritative, my commentary is not. Concern for absolute fidelity to his intent has pushed me to original sources and to all the checking procedures I know. But if there is distortion I am not only open, but eager, for correction. Similarly, I must be alone responsible for interpretations of the other materials alluded to throughout.

But nothing here is wilfully obscure. And it should be recognized that simplicity is not superficiality. The idea of a forever forward is not more or less simple than that of a forever backward. Yet, in our culture, one idea is commonplace, the other startling, even "unthinkable." (This retreat, it seems to me, is unavailable to those who say they understand the idea when it is applied to God.) My point is that there are deeps in man, and in the attempt to plumb him, depths which tax the most disciplined of minds, as also, which is much more, the most enlightened souls. I am with those who wish for a larger cup to grasp the ocean. But the Prophet, who was superb in making "the broad expanse of eternity" intelligible, warned that we do not enlarge the cup by a snap of the finger nor by a "fanciful, flowery and heated imagination;" only, he said, "by careful and ponderous and solemn thoughts." "By contrarieties," he added, "truth is made manifest."

A related kind of authority is needed in this realm. It is what, in the vernacular, is called "room to talk." It is hard come by. Academies help some, but life helps more.

The difference was all too graphic when I sat in the surgical chair of a Cambridge oculist. He asked me searching questions about the article on evil and suffering while he scraped at my eye. The pain was sharper than his instruments, and as I concentrated, or tried to, the thought recurred (familiar to most of us?) that I could stand both kinds of thrusts anywhere but there and then.

Personally, I think that any view of man that does not make a difference in such an ordeal, or in those compared to which this was a fleeting pin prick, is worthless. But it is only a rootless prejudice of our time that morbidity is profundity, and that any insight that seems consoling is bound to be a wishful and vagrant bromide. (The crutch of the immoralist is often his wishful disbelief.) It doesn't matter that I have had enough experience to be safe from confusing the Garden of Eden and the Garden of Gethsemane. What matters is that Christ and his prophets are, in all history, those most immersed in these realities and therefore in ours. If I had not known that self-understanding on the scale Christ had it, and through Him others, can endow life — all of it — with glorious meaning, these articles would never have been begun.

TRUMAN G. MADSEN

Contents

			PAGE
	Introduction		vi
	Preface		viii
CHAPTER I	WHENCE COMETH MAN ???		13
CHAPTER II	IDENTITY OR NOTHING		23
CHAPTER III	CREATION AND PROCREATION		34
CHAPTER IV	THE SPIRIT AND THE BODY		43
CHAPTER V	EVIL AND SUFFERING		53
CHAPTER VI	FREEDOM AND FULFILLMENT		63
CHAPTER VII	REVELATION AND SELF-REVELATION		71
	Index		78

Whence Cometh Man???

The great thing for us to know is to comprehend what God did institute before the foundation of the world. Who knows it?[1]

CHAPTER I

MODERN REVELATION, said the Prophet Joseph Smith, establishes "a foundation that will revolutionize the whole world."[2]

No insights, no set of flashes, are more revolutionary to the axioms of religion in the Western world than these three:

A. Man and woman are not derived from a void. They are beginningless. Their primal existence, as uncreated and indestructible intelligences, is everlasting.[3]

B. The "creation" of spirit or soul is not a fiat act at the time of mortal conception or birth. It is really Divine procreation in a world of glory.[4]

C. Physical birth in mortality is not totally at the initiative of God the Father. It is in part the result of premortal, individual election and foresight which are in harmony with uncreated law.[5]

Within the Church two opposite positions sometimes prevail about such ideas. One position assumes that they are so remote and incomplete that a "practical" man avoids thinking about them. The other assumes that by mere reference to pre-existence one can "explain" all events and eventualities.

The acceptance of these statements as ultimately true has immense consequences. To illustrate, here are several puzzles in philosophy and theology, along with glimpses of implied answers and their bearings:

1. The problem of human identity posed by Heraclitus and Hume, and by modern biology and physiology.[6]

2. The paradoxes of creation posed by Augustine and Thomas Aquinas.[7]

3. The mind-body problem posed by Descartes and by present-day cybernetics.[8]

---

[1]Smith, Joseph Fielding, ed., Teachings of the Prophet Joseph Smith, 1958 edition; Deseret Book Company, Salt Lake City, Utah; page 320.

[2]Ibid., page 366.

[3]"The intelligence of spirits had no beginning, neither will it have an end. That is good logic." Ibid., page 353. "Intelligence is eternal and exists upon a self-existent principle." Ibid., page 354. Compare Doctrine and Covenants 93:29, 30.

[4]"Element had an existence from the time He had. The pure principles of element are principles which can never be destroyed; they may be organized; and reorganized, but not destroyed. They had no beginning and can have no end." Ibid., pages 352, 301.

[5]Ibid., page 325. "The organization of spiritual and heavenly worlds, and of spiritual and heavenly beings, was agreeable to the most perfect order and harmony; their limits and bounds were fixed irrevocably, and voluntarily subscribed to in their heavenly estate by themselves . . ." (Italics added.)

[6]W. K. C. Guthrie, History of Greek Philosophy, Cambridge University Press, 1962, Vol. 1.

[7]See Basic Writings of St. Augustine, New York, Random House, 1948.

[8]N. Kemp Smith, New Studies in the Philosophy of Descartes, New York, Macmillan, 1952.

4. The problem of human freedom posed by Greek fatalism and teleology and by present-day psychoanalysis.[9]

5. The problem of evil or suffering posed by Job, Leibnitz, and so-called existenz-philosophy.[10]

6. The problem of self-awareness posed by Plato, and in our day by Jung; and all approaches to the "depth self."[11]

These are issues with complexities foreign to the layman. But each of us has convictions on these questions under less technical labels. And our whole life, conscious and subconscious, is colored by them.

Let us turn now to patterns of ordinary reflection and put them in personal terms, as if they arose (as they do) from some of the abiding anxieties of life:

1. The Problem of Identity (Developed in chapter 2)

Might I cease to be? Is there anything permanent in me? Am I, as Hume had it, "a bundle of perceptions," or as Russell says, "an accidental collocation of atoms"?[12]

Your conscious and purposive existence is guaranteed forever. The elements composing your intelligence, your begotten spirit and mortal body, are indestructible. Through stages, either of growth or degeneration, selfhood remains. Both utter extinction and permanent regression to a prior state are impossibilities.

Hence we are not, contrary to literary lamentations about the "predicament of man," suspended over "the abyss of non-

---

9See "Free Will and Responsibility" in Hospers and Sellars (eds.), *Readings in Ethical Theory*, New York, Appleton, 1952.

10See Book of Job. Leibnitz solution or "Theodicy" is presented in *Theodicy*. G. W. Leibnitz, London, Routledge & Kegan Paul Ltd., 1951, page 123.

11See Plato's dialogue *The Meno* where the pre-existent knowledge of the soul is demonstrated by a slave-boy's recollection of mathematical knowledge which he could not have apprehended in this world.

12Russell uses this phrase in his famous essay, "A Free Man's Worship." See "Russell's Philosophy of Religion" in *The Philosophy of Bertrand Russell*. Evanston, Illinois Library of Living Philosophers, 1946.

being."[13] Kierkegaard, Sartre, and Marcel are mistaken.[14] The only sense in which one can fail to *be* is in not realizing his full potential. His fundamental existence is not, and never will be, in jeopardy.

2. The Paradoxes of Creation (Developed in chapter 3)

How can I be anything except what God made me? How could an unchanging, immaterial First Cause bring a tangible me into being "ex nihilo" (from nothing)?

There is no creation "from nothing." There *is* ordering of elements: movement from simple to complex; growth from one degree to a greater degree, and from part to whole.

You are not just a product; you are an originator. In space you are coexistent with God. In time you are coeternal with God.

This view contradicts not only Sartre and Berdyaev on self-creation,[15] but also the Calvinistic concept of absolute pre-causation of all realities. It vitiates the dualism of material and immaterial, of firsts and derivatives.[16] (We are all "firsts.") It invalidates all of Thomas Aquinas' classical arguments for God based on "contingency."[17] And it solves Augustine's difficulty, bristling with contradictions, about when and where time and

---

[13]This is one of the recurring themes of existentialism — the threat of nothingness. See Kurt Reinhardt's *The Existentialist Revolt*, Milwaukee, The Bruce Publishing Company, 1952.

[14]Kierkegaard pleads for a leap of faith to the Absolute. Sartre pleads for the recognition, with Nietzsche, that "God is dead." Marcel turns to the Thomistic answer.

[15]Sartre's idea of freedom is sketched in his *L'Etre et le Neant*, page 127-130. Berdyaev's is outlined in *Zeitschrift fur philosophische Forschung*, Vol. VI, page 86ff. Calvinistic predetermination is taught in *The Institutes*. See *Calvin Theological Treatises*, Philadelphia Westminster Press, 1954, page 179.

[16]The view that the immaterial is utterly different from the material, and that the latter is utterly dependent on the former pervades almost every book on Christian theology or philosophy. Thomas assumes both that there must be a First Cause and that there can only be *one* First. Joseph Smith rejected these assumptions. See *Introduction to Saint Thomas Aquinas*, New York, Modern Library.

[17]The difficulties of Thomas' position are summarized in "The Existence of God," in *New Essays in Philosophical Theology*, ed. Flew and Macintyre, New York, Macmillan, 1955. See Truman G. Madsen's, "Joseph Smith and the Ways of Knowing," *B.Y.U. Seminar on Joseph Smith*, B.Y.U. Extension Publications, 1961, pages 36-37.

space were created. (Answer: They were not created but have always been in existence.)

3. The Mind-body Problem (Developed in chapter 4)

Which part of me is dominant or most important? Is mind reducible to matter, or matter to mind?

All three modes of your being — intelligence, spirit, and body — are essential to your self-fulfillment. Perfection of any one requires inseparable union with the others. God Himself is God because of His tripartite perfection.[18]

Gilbert Ryle's attack on the idea of an evanescent "ghost in the machine" is well-taken, but for reasons that he does not understand. The spirit is not a ghost, but a material entity.[19] The body is not a machine but an organic, purposive being. Interaction of these self-elements is far less problematic if (as is the case) they are similar in nature and not, as Descartes assumed, radically different.

Hence disparagements of intellect, mystical denials of the reality of the material world and religious or ethical castigations of the human body as utterly evil, here show up for what they are: extremes and delusions.[20]

4. The Problem of Human Freedom (Developed in chapter 5)

What are my capacities? Am I victimized by the circumstances of being badly born or badly conditioned?

Your autobiographical thread leads backward through the lineage of Deity and on to the original individual unit called 'intelligence." In it, in miniature, is the acorn of your potential oak, the unsculptured image of a glorified personality.

Freedom was not created. You are, and always will be, independent in that stage of development to which your volun-

---

18See Madsen's "Joseph Smith and the Problems of Ethics," *B.Y.U. Seminar on Joseph Smith*, B.Y.U. Extension Publications, 1962, Section 6, "The Nature of the Good Self."

19Gilbert Ryle, *The Concept of Mind*, London, Hutchinson, 1949.

20Today the constant phrase is that God is "wholly other," "utterly transcendent," or "absolutely unconditioned." Whenever religion has moved in this direction it has tended, likewise, to minimize man. "Finite," "demonic," "depraved," are typical of dominant trends.

tary decisions and divine powers have led. There are limits all along the way to what you can be and do. But you are not a billiard ball. No power in the universe can coerce your complete assent or dissent.

This thesis on capacity dissolves the absolute wall that Western theologians have erected between Deity and man.[21] It increases the awe one feels in the superlative motives that led God the Father and Jesus the Christ to glorify not "things" of their absolute make, but persons who were part of their everlasting environment. It translates Bergson's metaphor into breath-taking fact, "The universe is a machine for the making of gods."[22]

The freedom thesis undercuts the causal dogmas of behaviorists, mechanists, fatalists, and predestinationists. John Wisdom has lately argued that one can only justify a belief in free agency by a belief in pre-existence.[23] The identification of freedom with primal intelligence does just that.

5. The Problem of Evil, of Suffering (Developed in chapter 6)

How can we account for inequalities? And how can God be good and powerful and yet permit human suffering?

God is responsible neither for the innate limits of uncreated element nor for the eternal and inviolate principles within which the Gospel plan is instituted. By application of these, not by a cosmic accident, He became what He is. Likewise He aids all of us in reaching our fulness.

Thus, it is not a "decree" that stress and pain are part of growth and enlightenment. The universe and the selves within it simply operate that way. It is enough to know that God the Father and His Son Jesus Christ, though not the source of tragedy, yet have power to enable us to climb above it, into everlasting joy.

---

[21]Is there not a deeper root of love in us for a Father who lifts us by His own love and power, than for a Fiat Creator who brought us into being from nothing?

[22]Henri Bergson, *The Two Sources of Morality and Religion,* New York Holt and Company, 1935, last page.

[23]John Wisdom, *Philosophy and Psychoanalysis,* Oxford Blackwell, 1953.

As to present ills, we anticipated them. Yet we chose, and chose with knowledge, these very conditions and risks. In a word, we were not, contrary to French nihilists, "thrown" into the world. Every mortal, to reverse' the popular statement, did "ask to be born." (And those who say they are in their second childhood unwittingly speak the truth.) We might have avoided mortality. Billions did, and thus drastically limited their possibilities.

This position abandons the classical dilemma of the nature and meaning of the soul's creation. It does not rest, with Edwards, on "the inscrutable will of God."[24] It exonerates God from "man's inhumanity to man." It parallels Brightman's notion of "the Given" with which God is struggling, willing the ultimate happiness for all His creatures.[25] It refutes the view of a Bradley or a Buddha that evil is illusory.[26] It breaks out of the triangle argument that God cannot be both all-good and all-powerful, by showing that God is Himself operating within eternal limits.[27]

6. The Problem of Self-awareness (Developed in chapter 7)

How can I know my real self?

Your maximum unfolding depends partly on not yet knowing your infinite past; but also it depends on knowing what is deepest in you, while in mortality.

---

[24]The phrase is also central in Calvin. Not only is God inscrutable but we sin if we seek to understand God. God is "essential mystery," not simply a not-yet-known but an unknowable. In contrast Joseph Smith wrote, "The day shall come when you shall comprehend even God, being quickened in him and by him." Doctrine and Covenants 88:49.

[25]Edgar Sheffield Brightman in A Philosophy of Religion, New York, Prentice-Hall, 1940. Brightman is also convinced that God must be a personal being, and that the greatest coherence of human experience and observation confirms this. In this he stands with a minority of present-day writers on religion.

[26]Both Christian Science and Oriental thought affirm that evil is appearance, not reality; that suffering is an illusion. Joseph Smith taught that suffering is real, but meaningful and purposive. His view is "instrumental." See Doctrine and Covenants 122.

[27]The argument is that if God permits suffering because he cannot prevent it then He is not all-powerful. If He permits suffering though He could prevent it, then he is not all good. The standard reply is that God must allow suffering in order to allow freedom. But, again, if He were all-powerful, He could guarantee freedom without suffering. Joseph Smith revealed that God is himself surrounded by everlasting law, eternal intelligences; hence eternal conditions. He became God by abiding these conditions. He did not create, neither can He destroy them.

Such a learning process recollects more than it researches.
It is the opposite of amnesia. It is less discovery than recovery.
(And every religious teacher should, in this realm, conceive
his role as the Master Teacher and Socrates did: as a midwife
of ideas, not as their transplanter.)

One begins mortality with the veil drawn, but slowly he is
moved to penetrate the veil within himself. He is, in time, led
to seek the "holy of holies" within the temple of his own being.

The dawning of the light has three main sources:

First, there is inspired introspection. As we move through
life, half-defined recollections and faint but sometimes vivid
outlines combine to bring a familiar tone or ring to our experience.

One feels at times at home in a universe which, for all that
is grotesque and bitter, yet has meaning. Wordsworth called
this a "presence that disturbs me with the joy of elevated
thoughts. A sense sublime of something far more deeply inter-
fused."[28]

One recognizes as Fromm and Rogers and others describe
it, "What one authentically *is*."[29] At times he feels, with William James, like "the real me," "most alive."[30] One feels he is
on a path anticipated or prepared for, in part a prefabricated
path. Rufus Jones calls this "the luminous trail."[31]

One has sacred moments in relation to persons, places, and
situations which bear the subtle stamp of prior awareness, however elusive. Rudolph Otto calls this (in Latin) "*a priori* nu-
minousness."[32] One hears truths expressed, "hidden from before
the foundation of the world," and is pulled to them with over-

[28]William Wordsworth, *Tintern Abbey. Complete Poetical Works*, London,
Macmillan, 1890.

[29]Carl Rogers, *Counseling and Psychotherapy*, New York, Houghton Mifflin
Co., 1942.

[30]William James, *Principles of Psychology*, Volume I, page 299, New York,
Holt, 1890. See also *The Three Jameses*, C. H. Grattan, London, Longmans Green
& Co., 1932 page 225. "At such moments there is a voice inside which speaks
and says: 'This is the real me.' "

[31]Rufus Jones in *A Call to What Is Vital*, New York, Macmillan, 1948.

[32]Rudolph Otto, *Idea of the Holy*, Oxford University Press, 1923. The word
"numinous" is a derivative of "luminous." It depicts, for Otto, the deep and
latent response to sacred things.

whelming gratitude. Jesus Christ, who promised He would bring all things to our remembrance, defined all this and more when He said, "My sheep know my voice."[33]

Second, beyond these inner hints recognized by poets and philosophers are the revelations of the prophets. Like a physician to a patient who has "lost" his memory they say:

"You were at the first organization in heaven.[34] You saw the Savior chosen and appointed, and the plan of life presented; and you sanctioned it.[35] You were a participant in a grand council when specific mortal missions were assigned and 'were ordained to that very calling.'[36] You were present at the creation of the earth and took your place in the organization of the human family."[37] Illumined, these statements can change from cold conceptions or thoughts to warm realities.

But, *third*, there are the concrete and individual pronouncements of the patriarch who has been called to stand between heaven and earth. His inspiration may reach from the celestial hearth to earthly heritage, and from the vital promises of mission to the morning of divine reunion — and beyond. No "Whence came I?" and no "Who am I?" receive such a transforming answer as this leaf from the eternal diary.

Now, none of these "ways" is scientifically operational. Even if, as Jung thought, most psychic illness is rooted in religious maladjustment; even if glimpses of the "collective unconscious" can help resolve it, these glimpses are not laboratory-induced.[38] Traces of ourselves show up in inkblot tests, in free association, in dreams, in parapsychology. But always there is more, awaiting the visitation of the Perfect Psychiatrist.

33Joseph F. Smith, "Spirit Memories," in *Gospel Doctrine*, Salt Lake City, Utah, Deseret Book Company, 12th Edition, 1961, page 13. "All those salient truths which come home so forcibly to the head and heart seem but the awakening of the memories of the spirit."

34*Teachings of the Prophet Joseph Smith*, page 181.

35*Ibid.*, pages 181, 308.

36*Ibid.*, pages 190, 220, 365.

37*Ibid.*, page 158.

38See Carl B. Jung, *Modern Man in Seach of a Soul*, New York, Harcourt Brace & Co., 1934.

Enough has now been said to establish the point that not only does awareness of the pre-existence make a difference, but that it is a prodigious difference.

For it follows from all this that no philosophy or psychology of personality, no attempt to speak accurately about the nature of the mental, the spiritual, or the physical, no solution to questions on the meaning of life, in sum, no approach to any question bearing on the origins or destiny of man (and all questions eventually lead to these), can be adequate without taking account of these six answers.

Modern man has penetrated the self and found much that is shocking and unspeakably dark. By a Freud, a Niebuhr, a Heidegger, the viper within man has been widely heralded.[39] But this, for all its professed depth, has been too shallow.

For deeper still, *in* and not just *below* all in man that needs healing and redeeming, are the remnants and rudiments of glory. As one uncovers that level he recognizes not one but two; not just his depths but his heights, not just himself but God.

And that is a syllable of meaning in one of the most profound statements ever made about man. It was given by Joseph Smith:

> If men do not comprehend the character of God,
> they do not comprehend themselves.[40]

What, then, of the man who really comprehends himself?

---

[39]Heidegger in philosophy has shown the depths of a man's guilt and "angst" (anguish). Freud in psychology has uncovered the riotous impulses of the sub-conscious. Niebuhr in theology has shown man victimized by the "Fall," the symbol of sins of pride and self-assurance.

[40]*Teachings of the Prophet Joseph Smith*, page 343.

Identity
or Nothing

When things that are of the greatest importance are passed over by weak-minded men without even a thought, I want to see truth in all its bearings and hug it to my bosom.[1]

— Joseph Smith.

CHAPTER II

I F THE ANCIENT saying "Know Thyself" is a primary human aim, then "Seek Thine Origins" is surely a part of it.

Regarding the ultimate identity of man, the Prophet Joseph Smith taught that man as a primal intelligence is eternal. Likewise the spirit-elements that compose his Divinely-sired spirit and the matter-elements that compose his physically-sired

[1]Smith, Joseph Fielding (editor), *Teachings of the Prophet Joseph Smith*, Deseret News Press, Salt Lake City, Utah, 1958 edition; page 374.

body are eternal. Except in procreation, these elements of the total self never become an *essential* part of any other self. Once united, their destiny is to be glorified and "inseparably connected" throughout all eternity.

My task is not to argue for or against this concept of personal eternalism.[2] Nor is it to examine the credentials which would be presented if the questions were raised, "Why is this believed?" or "How is this known?" Instead: Suppose this *is* the truth about man — what does it mean, and what follows? What are some important consequences of accepting this idea in the contemporary world?

Four Characterizations

To begin with, what does Joseph Smith's affirmation about intelligences really say? Let us agree at the outset that much is left indeterminate.[3] But does not a careful reading require at least these four characterizations?[4]

Individuality. Man as a self had a beginningless beginning. He has never been identified wholly with any other being. Nor is he a product of nothing. "Intelligence is eternal and exists upon a self-existent principle. . . . There is no creation about it."[5]

---

[2]The term "eternalism" was coined by B. H. Roberts to describe the Mormon position. See Roberts, B. H., *Comprehensive History of the Church*, Deseret News Press, Salt Lake City, Utah, 1930; page 410.

[3]Fascinating questions, for example, immediately arise about the unoriginated status, differences, "gifts," talents, and capacities of intelligences. On these issues there are only hints in the Prophet's teachings.

[4]Another attempt to do this is in the paper, "Joseph Smith and the Problem of Ethics," Joseph Smith Seminar, 1962; Brigham Young University Extension Publications, Provo, Utah.

[5]*Teachings of the Prophet Joseph Smith*, page 354. Individuality is difficult to picture. That has led some to the view that "intelligence" is a name given to a primal stuff out of which, perhaps, the spirit personality is constructed, but that individuality does not really emerge until then. The doctrine of the Church, however, is clearly a doctrine of individual, separate intelligences. This is required by the original statements of the Prophet in Nauvoo. The *Journal of Wilford Woodruff*, for example, shows that the phrase "a spirit from age to age" refers to an entity, a person, an individual. (See footnotes to the sermon in *Teachings*, especially p. 354). It is required by the logic of the Prophet "Anything that has a beginning may have an end." It is required by the use of the plural "intelligences" in many passages in the Standard Works. Finally, it is required by official pronouncements of the Church. The issue became a matter of wide discussion in the early 1900's. B. H. Roberts' *Seventy's Yearbook*, Volume 4, assumed the co-eternity of individuals. The book was read and approved by the First Council of the Seventy. Later controversy resulted in an article titled "The Immortality of Man." By assignment, Elder Roberts read this article first to President Francis M. Lyman, then

Autonomy. The self is free. All intelligence ". . . is independent in that sphere in which God has placed it, to act for itself . . . otherwise there is no existence."[6]

Consciousness. There is no inanimate intelligence or unconscious mind. These are contradictions in terms. Selfhood and individual consciousness are unending. "The intelligence of spirits had no beginning, neither will it have an end. That is good logic. That which has a beginning may have an end."[7]

Capacity for Development. "All the minds and spirits that God ever sent into the world are susceptible of enlargement."[8]

The Shaking of Foundations

Few of us may realize how radical these theses are in contrast to dominant assumptions of our time.

I once presented to some graduate students the idea that man's intelligence was unoriginated and indestructible. That was in a Harvard Seminar on Augustine.[9] The entire class was violent in its outbursts. For some minutes the professor's anxiety to keep the peace was futile.

Why is the idea so staggering? Because it not only challenges established religious dogmas about man, but also leading secular viewpoints. It uproots in one fell swoop presuppositions that are lodged in billions of minds and millions of books. The notion today is more revolutionary than would be the revision of all mathematical operations of men and machines on the discovery that one and one do not make two, but infinity.

---

to the First Presidency (President Joseph F. Smith was President) and seven of the Council of the Twelve. It was thoroughly discussed. The article was published with their encouragement and endorsement. (April, 1907 *Improvement Era*). This article teaches the "existence of independent, uncreated, self-existent intelligences" which, though they differ, are "alike in their eternity and their freedom." (p. 419). This is a doctrine, Roberts often said, "from which spring most glorious and harmonious truths."

[6]Doctrine and Covenants 93:29. I interpolate cautiously that the meaning here is "Otherwise there is no existence of *selves*" distinct from inanimate reality. If *all* existence depends on the independence of intelligence we have idealism instead of realism.

[7]*Teachings of the Prophet Joseph Smith*, page 353.

[8]*Ibid.*, page 354.

[9]The question arose in discussing the issues of predeterminism in Augustine's conception of creation.

Likewise, as I have said elsewhere,[10] these ideas are so pervasive in their implications that every question that pertains to man is related to them.

Rewarding Rewording

Even Latter-day Saints, when the idea is put in ways that break out of routine phraseology, may find that it shakes their ordinary ways of thinking. Here, for example, are some of its meanings and entailments:

The quantity, though not the quality, of selves is fixed forever. It is infinite.

There is no beginning to our "beginning."

Mind has no birthday and memory has no first.

Age is relative only to stages, not existence. No one is older, or younger, than anyone else.

We have always been alone, separate from, and always together, coexistent with, other intelligences.

Creation is never totally original; it is always a combination of prior realities.

Immortality is in no sense conditional. It is inevitable and universal, even for sub-human intelligences.

Whatever may be said of the spirit and body, death does not destroy the self, but only delimits it.

Death, like all events, is lived through. It is comparable to the loss of an arm, and that is temporary.

Suicide is just a change of scenery.

Through all transformations of eternity, no self can change completely into another thing. Identity remains.

In an ultimate sense, no existent self ever loses his mind nor his consciousness.

In sum, nothing is something we never were and never can be.

Three Contrasting Outlooks

Let us turn now to three contrasting outlooks:

---

[10]In the article "Whence Cometh Man," *Instructor*, June, 1963.

1. *Orthodox Christendom*

For the traditionated Christian, man is derived from nothing or from nonbeing by the fiat act of God. The Divine created *ex nihilo*[11] (out of nothing) both the soul and body of man, which is to say, the whole of man. Indeed, everything except God is derived from nonbeing.

Man, in this view, becomes the proof of God, for since man is absolutely contingent (he would not be except for something outside himself), we must conclude that something created him and that something must be absolutely necessary or self-existent. St. Thomas and his heirs, with faith, not, as claimed, with logic, move from that something to Something and from Something to the Christian God.[12]

Allied with this view is the notion of God's continual creation. God is the "sustainer" of man and of all reality. Without God there would be no other being; hence, He is "being-itself." This has tended repeatedly in Christian theology to limit or even deny man's freedom and certainly his enlargement. For if God is directly responsible for all that man is, He is indirectly responsible for all that man does.[13]Calvin faced this consequence squarely. Denying freedom, he held that all acts of men are acts of God, even the sinking of the murderer's knife into the victim's back.[14] Others have held that God created man totally for His purpose, yet that man is responsible for his salvation and is not a pawn.[15]

11The official definition of "creation ex nihilo" is, "God brings the entire substance of a thing into existence from a state of nonexistence. . . . What is peculiar to creation is the entire absence of any prior subject-matter," *Catholic Encyclopedia*, Volume IV, Robert Appleton, New York, 1908; page 470.

12See *Introduction to Saint Thomas Aquinas*, Modern Library New York, page 709. That God is self-existent is correct enough. But, asks the Prophet, "Who told you that man does not exist in like manner on the same principles? Man does exist on the same principles," *Teachings of the Prophet Joseph Smith*, page 352.

13And this is the problem of God-and-evil (theo-dike, theodicy). It remains the strongest secular objection to belief in a purposive and worthy Deity.

14See critical commentary in Anthony Flew, "Divine Omnipotence and Human Freedom," *New Essays in Philosophical Theology*, Flew & Macintyre (editors); Macmillan, New York, 1955.

15Modern and liberal theology have emphasized the intrinsic worth and dignity of man and significantly have reinstated purpose, creative personality, heightened consciousness, and expanded opportunities in the life to come. But the present trend is a landslide toward a pessimistic disparagement of man. See Dillenberger and Welch (editors) *Protestant Christianity; Scribner's*, New York, 1954.

Christian theology qualifies the individuality and consciousness of man. Man may be swallowed up in the "Absolute Principle";[16] or his consciousness may cease at death;[17] or he may be subject to a conditional resurrection; or, (as in Eastern religion) he may be cast in a radically different form into a more ethereal realm.[18]

In sum: creation is the absolute mysterious act of God; freedom is foreshortened or denied; and consciousness and enlargement opportunities are focused on mortality. (Few Christians believe either in a premortal self or in salvation opportunities beyond mortal death.)

The orthodox Christian attitude toward life is a faith-state submission to the inscrutable will of God and faith in a purposeful fulfillment beyond the grave. He trusts that God is good and His creation of man meaningful. He is willing, whatever he may be, to be.

2. Existentialism

For existentialism, man is a derivative of nothing, is now almost nothing, and is destined for nothing.

"Existentialism" is the unpronounceable name of a doctrine advanced by a group, some religious, some a-religious, of European origin.[19] It is now one of the most influential movements in the Western world. These writers are in the lineage of Job, Augustine, and Pascal.[20] After the most agonizing studies in self-scrutiny, they conclude that man is a phantom, a "useless passion," to use Sartre's phrase.[21]

Some of these writers account for man as self-creating. (It requires tremendously complex analysis to show how a non-

---

[16]See an outline of different positions in E. S. Brightman, A Philosophy of Religion; Prentice-Hall, New York, 1940.

[17]This view for some sects is called "soul-sleeping."

[18]Eastern religion, e.g., Buddhism, aspires to absolute annihilation of the soul. Many Christians hope for the annihilation, or at least escape from, the body; hence do not believe in the resurrection.

[19]Barrett, William, Irrational Man; Doubleday, Garden City, 1958.

.[20]See "The Contribution of Existentialism," by Truman G. Madsen, BYU Studies, Winter 1959. (A synopsis is in the Proceedings of the Utah Academy of Arts and Sciences, 1959.)

[21]See The Philosophy of Existentialism, Gabriel Marcel; Citadel Press, New York, 1962.

existent self can create an existent self; and then lack the power to perpetuate it.)[22] The main approach is not to man viewed from the outside, but from the inside. Such inner realities as anxiety, dread, guilt, suffering, monotony, nausea, despair are portrayed in excruciating detail.[23] The starkest, darkest threat of all is, paradoxically, nothing. Man is under the "threat of nonbeing," the ontological shock of "I might not be." Man is absolute finitude; and life, as Kierkegaard states it, is "the sickness unto death."[24] This is the "abyss" beneath the surface, the "limit-encounter" to rephrase Jaspers, which destroys security, destroys meaning, and haunts our identity until we are swallowed in its chasm. More than the fear of death, this is the anguish of absolute negation.[25]

In sum: creation is a mystery of self-propulsion; freedom is absolute except in overcoming the "limit" of being; consciousness is agony; and "enlargement" is meaningless.

The existentialist attitude toward life is utter pessimism. Suicide is its most consistent outcome. Answerable to nobody and estranged from everybody, these people suffer through the disease of "nihilism." Even those who follow Kierkegaard or Marcel or Tillich and "leap" to God, leap in the dark and are convinced that "Before God we are always in the wrong."[26] At best "eternal life" is a symbol for enduring in the present sordid world.[27] This is a religion of much nothing and nothing much.

22Berdyaev and Sartre are among the number. Sartre's great tome, L' Etre et le Neant (Being and Nothing) treats this subject at length.

23The very titles of their books reflect chronic melancholy: Kierkegaard's, Fear and Trembling; Sartre's, Flies, No Exit, Troubled Sleep; Unamuno's, Tragic Sense of Life.

24See Tillich's account in his Systematic Theology, Volume II, Introduction; University of Chicago Press, Chicago, 1958.

25Collins, James, The Existentialists, presents this under "Five Existentialists Themes"; Regnery, Chicago, 1959.

26So says Kierkegaard. See Dorothy Emmet's treatment of this in connection with Barth, Brunner, and Niebuhr in The Nature of Metaphysical Thinking; Macmillan, London, 1949; chapter VI.

27So Desan titles his treatment of Sartre, The Tragic Finale; Cambridge, Harvard University Press, 1954.

3. *Humanism*

For Humanists, man comes from something and returns to something. But this something is "cosmic dust," which is almost nothing.[28]

In close alliance with present scientific method and findings, humanists try to account for man as an "epiphenomenon"; man is to the cosmos what a train whistle is to the train.[29] If "explanations" are necessary, a blend of Darwin and microbiology may be invoked.[30]Matter or matter-energy came first, then one-celled organisms, then consciousness and the so-called "higher" human traits. Mind is an accident. It will not last long before its reduction to matter. The body is a collection of atoms whose turnover is complete every seven years, and whose disorganization is imminent.[31]

Man, on this view, is a temporary event, a fleeting figure in the blind careenings of the cosmos. (There is, of course, no reference to God.) His identity is soon to be obliterated, and with it all of his expressions of beauty, goodness, knowledge, and love. All will be swallowed up in what Russell calls "the vast death of the solar system."[32] So when Wernher von Braun tries to bolster hopes for personal immortality by saying "nothing disappears without a trace,"[33] the humanist agrees; but the trace will not be conscious. As Montague has it, the things that matter most will ultimately be at the mercy of the things that matter least.[34]

In sum: creation is a shifting of molecules; freedom is a name for our ignorance of the causes that determine us; con-

---

[28]See Corliss Lamont, *Humanism as a Philosophy;* Philosophical Library, New York, 1949.

[29]The point of the comparison is that the train whistle has no substantial character of its own, but disappears even if the train does not.

[30]See, for instance, George Wald, "The Origin of Life," in *The Physics and Chemistry of Life;* Scientific American Booklet, 1955.

[31]See Corliss Lamont, *The Illusion of Immortality;* G. P. Putnam and Sons, New York, 1935.

[32]Russell, Bertrand, "A Free Man's Worship," in *Mysticism and Logic;* Doubleday Anchor, New York, 1957.

[33]Von Braun is featured in the BYU Science and Religion film and restates what he said in a feature article in the "This Week" magazine section.

[34]So William Peperell Montague says in *Belief Unbound;* Yale University Press, New Haven, 1930.

sciousness is a flicker; and "enlargement" is a start before a final stop.

The humanist attitude toward life is, unlike the existentialist, affirmative. But unlike the Christian, it is altogether "this-worldly." He lives prudently, grateful for pleasures, patient in pain. He is not an absolute pessimist. There are still worthwhile dreams, hopes, and achievements. He is a kind of stoic, pursuing ends he believes will soon come to nothing.

Now, with these viewpoints as background, let the Latter-day Saints re-read and contrast Joseph Smith's theses on identity. Let him trace their incompatibility with these prevailing outlooks. And let him ask himself how they color his attitudes toward life, in ways far more numerous than this outline conveys.

The Nothingness of Nothing

To speak logically and summarily, if the New Dispensation doctrine be true, then these three positions on the origins and identity of man are false. The orthodox Christian, the existentialist, and the humanist are asking themselves, with Hamlet, a pseudo-question: "To be or not to be?" That is *not* the question.[35] No one can choose to be or not to be. Nor can anything in the universe make anyone be or not be. Everyone simply and eternally *is* an individual, free, conscious, enlargeable self.

If the question is pointless, then so is the colossus of anxieties and efforts that revolve around it. *Nothing* is not the source of, not a threat to, and not the destiny of man. Any religion or doctrine of man that is haunted by *Nothing* is really haunted by nothing at all.

It necessarily follows that the orthodox Christian worships, (and some Christians condemn) God for an impossible ex nihilo creation. This He did not and could not do. The existentialist laments in total anguish the threat of nonbeing. But there is no

---

35Hamlet, of course, was really speaking of the choice between living and dying. He found the alternative of death, and the unknown beyond it, less desirable than facing his "sea of troubles." With many men today, it is the other way around.

such threat. The humanist lives with hasty heroism to achieve a few satisfactions before cosmic oblivion. But such oblivion will never come.

All three movements hold theses on man's individuality, freedom, consciousness, and enlargement that cannot be logically squared with the Prophet's teachings.

What *is* the question? The question is not one of being, but of becoming. "To become more or not to become more." This is the question faced by each intelligence in our universe. At this point, and not before, the absolute and inescapable need for God and His Christ arises. And those who choose are, in the declaration of the ancient prophet, Abraham, and in the language of the modern prophet, Joseph Smith, those who are "added upon."

Creation
and Procreation

*The immortal spirit. Where did it come from? All
learned men and doctors of divinity say that God created it in the beginning; but it is not so: the very idea
lessens man in my estimation. I do not believe the doctrine; I know better. Hear it, all ye ends of the world;
for God has told me so; and if you don't believe me, it
will not make the truth without effect. . . . I am going
to tell of things more noble.*

— *Joseph Smith, King Follet Discourse.*[1]

[1]*Teachings of the Prophet Joseph Smith*, compiled by Joseph Fielding Smith;
Deseret News Press, Salt Lake City, Utah, 1958 edition; page 352. B. H. Roberts
suggests that "immortal spirit" in this quotation refers to intelligence. Nevertheless, the remarks apply also to the begetting of the spirit.

33

CHAPTER III

I N HIS POETIC rewriting of one of the sublime visions of all time, the Prophet Joseph records:

And I heard a great voice bearing record from Heav'n,
He's the Saviour, and Only Begotten of God—
By him, of him, and through him, the worlds were all made,
Even all that career in the heavens so broad.

Whose inhabitants, too, from the first to the last,
Are sav'd by the very same Saviour of ours;
And, of course, are begotten God's daughters and sons, .
By the very same truths, and the very same pow'rs.[2]

Eternity is here sketched in eight lines. We select two marvelous themes: First, the worlds, world-systems, and galaxies, dazzling in brightness and dizzying in number, move under the creative mastery of Jesus Christ. Second, all spirits of the inhabitants of these worlds, including the spirit of Jesus Christ Himself, were not gotten from nothing but begotten of God; not created but procreated, sired by the supreme personality of our universe, God the Father.[3]

In a world of glory that could not be endured by mortal man; in realms, indeed, that ". . . surpass all understanding in glory, and in might, and in dominion, . . ."[4] the eternal intelligence of man was merged with eternal spirit-elements and began its enlargement in the presence of the Divine.

The Familiar and Familial

But is Divine fatherhood in any sense similar to human fatherhood?

The analogues are more profound than any Christian writer since the first century has dared to examine.[5] For our purpose

---

[2]*Times and Seasons*, Vol. IV, No. 6; February 1, 1843; pages 82-85.
[3]See Doctrine and Covenants 76:24.
[4]*Ibid.*, 76:114.
[5]Some of the early Christian fathers clearly recognized the distinction between creation and generation, between a thing created and a self-procreated. Athanasius, for one, says, "Let it be repeated that a created thing is external to the nature of

one all-important likeness must be named. It is unequivocally taught by the Prophet.

In mortal birth, inherent physical and personality traits of the father and mother are transmitted to their son or daughter. (A thimbleful of chromosomes accounts for the physical make-up and qualities of the billions who have so far inhabited this globe.) More, one's bodily inheritance and then his environment mold him and largely condition his destiny.

It is exactly so with man's spirit. Long before mortality, in a process of actual transmission, there were forged into man's spirit the embryonic traits, attributes, and powers of God Himself! And in the surroundings of that realm man was nurtured in the Divine image.[6]

Before we trace the transcendent religious power of this truth, let us consider it from the center of critical theological analysis. There are two entrenched objections to it. Rarely have they had such an array of influential advocates. Both of them have been impressed upon most of us.

First, anthropomorphism. The idea of fatherhood is objectionable because of its primitive and naive approach to biblical language. Phrases like Jesus' "My father" and "your father," or Paul's "offspring of God" and "Father of our spirits" must not be interpreted as literal.[7] To apply such manlike qualities to the Divine, and Godlike qualities to man, is to abase and abuse the message. Since the time of Maimonides in Judaism and Dionysius in Christianity it has been a commonplace that we must not ascribe finite categories to Deity.[8] "Fatherhood" con-

---

the being who creates; but a generation is the proper offspring of the nature" (of him who begets it). "Every son," he observes, "is co-essential or co-substantial with his father." But in later theology man is held to be "external to the nature of the being who creates," not a son. See William Greenough Thayer Shedd, *History of Christian Doctrine*, Vol. I; C. Scribner and Sons, New York; 1863; page 322.

6See the King Follett Discourse, *Teachings of the Prophet Joseph Smith*, pages 342-362.

7There are over a hundred occurrences of "father" and its variants in the four Gospels. See Paul's phrases in Acts 17 and Hebrews 12.

8On Maimonides see Ben Zion Bokser, *The Legacy of Maimonides*; Philosophical Library, New York, 1950. See also James M. Clark, *The Great Vesman Mystics*; Blackwell, Oxford, 1949.

notes materiality, subjection to space and time, and other absurdities. It destroys the dignity, majesty, and unconditioned ultimacy of God.[9]

Second, psychologism. The idea of fatherhood is objectionable because, as Freud tells us, all men tend to project (invent rather than discover) their "father-image."[10] "God the Father" is a paternal pie that is a lie in the sky. Adler says our inferiority feelings; Feuerbach, our childish wishes; Marx, our economic frustrations, are at the root of the projection.[11] We thus "personify" our subjective hopes to avoid reality.

Now quite apart from Joseph Smith and the modern prophets, there are telling rebuttals to these anxieties.

Milton saw the real issue. He was aware of the subtleties of language. And though he could not escape a whole canopy of now discredited assumptions in the 17th century, he claimed to be inspired in his poetry. The Bible, he says, is seriously literal in what it says about the fatherhood of God. There is no radical distinction between spirit and matter, and there is a point-by-point analogy between heaven and earth.[12] God is the actual sire of the souls of men. Why, he asks, should we be afraid to ascribe to God what He ascribes to Himself?[13]

Why indeed? The fear is especially inept in Christendom, which, by its most central thesis, is committed to the idea of Divine fatherhood. Every orthodox theologian must maintain that God was the immortal Father of Jesus. Jesus' actual Sonship accounts for the fact that He was, or became, "the express image of His (the Father's) person."[14] Mary, a human being,

---

[9]See Tillich's *Biblical Religion and the Search for Ultimate Reality;* University of Chicago Press, Chicago, 1955. See the near best seller by John A. T. Robinson, an Anglican Bishop, *Honest To God;* The Westminister Press, Philadelphia, 1963. It predicts the "end of theism" and the triumph of "being-itself."

[10]Freud, *The Future of an Illusion;* Leveright, 1953.

[11]Alfred Alder, *The Practice and Theory of Individual Psychology;* Routledge, London, 1955.

L. Feuerbach, *The Essence of Christianity* (English translation, 1854).

On Marx, see Erich Fromm, *Marx's Concept of Man;* Ungar, New York, 1961.

[12]See John Milton, *Paradise Lost;* and J. S. Whale, *Christian Doctrine,* VII; Cambridge University Press, London, 1963; beginning line 168.

[13]See J. S. Whale, *Christian Doctrine,* Book I; chapter 2.

[14]See Hebrews 1:1-3.

was the mother of the body of Christ.[15] Why should not God, a Divine being, be the father of the spirit of man? If one is unthinkable, so is the other. In principle it is absurd to maintain that God could, without losing His dignity, majesty, or ultimacy transmit a divine nature through a mortal being, and then say that He could not transmit spirit traits, in His likeness, to immortal spirits.[16]

The Conquest of Paradox

But the problem of the theologian is complex.

Behold the paradoxes that he presents as an alternative concept of creation:

The immaterial Trinity elicited from nothing both material and immaterial substance. The unchanging and unchangeable Deity yet changed and changes the whole of reality. A nontemporal and nonspatial being, literally nowhere and "nowhen," yet created and infused everywhere and "everywhen." The All-powerful and All-good simultaneously and yet continuously brought into being not only mankind, but the angels, the demons, and Satan. Moreover, like did not create like. Between the Divine and all other natures there was and is and always will be an absolute gulf.[17] Because man is utterly other than the Divine, his creation required mediators. Thus, through emanation or through angels who are "pure form" (bodiless and more than man yet less than God) or by the speaking of a cosmic word, man came into being.[18]

It is in vain to protest that these are radical contradictions. The creed-upholding Christian will reply, "Of course they are."

15But the idea of a radical dualism between Divine and human has led Roman Catholicism to first qualify and then deny Mary's humanity. By papal decrees she was held immune to original sin, then given the graces of the Spirit, then called "co-redemptress" or "co-mediator" with Christ, then declared to be "assumed" bodily into heaven without death; now the Vatican Council is deliberating on whether she shall be decreed a member of the Godhead. See *The Mary Book*, assembled by F. J. Sheed; Sheed and Ward, London and New York, 1950.

16See Note 5.

17See J. S. Whale, *Christian Doctrine*; Chapter I.

18Gilson summarizes the standard view: "The revealed notion of creation, (is) understood by believers and theologians alike as the absolute production of being from no other pre-existing condition than the free will of its creator." See *The Elements of Christian Philosophy*, Doubleday Press, New York, 1963; p. 181.

They belong to the mysteries of the Divine, and obviously the finite intellect cannot understand. Thus it is often held that to be mystified is to be edified, and that intellectual confusion is a religious virtue.[19]

The teachings of Joseph Smith, like those of the ancient prophets, are involved in *none* of these paradoxes.

Reverence or Irreverence

But what is the religious appeal of this outlook?

Significantly, the doctrine of an utterly transcendent God usually flourishes most in an era when humanity is shocked at its own demonic or depraved conduct. We live in such a time. Anything so tinctured with corruption, it is said, cannot be Divine. True enough. But almost without exception western theologians have taken this insight and pushed it to conclusions not only mistaken, but contrary to their original intent. Weighed down by the fact of degenerate parenthood, they are unable to conceive of Divine parenthood. Inveighing against the corruptions of mortal personality, they are unable to conceive of Divine personality. Hence, they conclude that God is neither a parent nor a person.

What is left? "Being-itself"; what Buber, Marcel, Barth, Niebuhr, and Tillich, representing the Jewish, Catholic, and Protestant traditions call "The Transcendent."[20]

But nothing in the universe is loftier than personality. All who look outside of it in quest of the Divine will find something lower. Calling it the "Unconditioned" in capital letters fails to deify, though it does idolize. Only by covertly ignoring

---

[19]See *Religious Experience and Truth*, a Symposium ed. by Sydney Hook; New York University Press, 1961; in which some logic-minded analysts confront the religious defenders of paradox, especially Part III.

[20]See Martin Buber's, *I and Thou*, Translated by R. G. Smith; Scribner's, New York, 1958.

Kegley, Bretall, (editors) *Reinhold Niebuhr*; Macmillan, New York, 1956.

Gustave Weigel's, "Myth, Symbol, and Analogy," in *Religion and Culture;* Harper's, New York, 1959; Chapter 9.

Rudolph Bultmann, *Kerygma and Myth*, H. W. Bartschr (editor), Volume I., London, S.P.C.K., 1953.

Paul Tillich, *Systematic Theology*, Volume I; University of Chicago Press, Chicago, 1965.

these theological restrictions and investing the concept with personal meaning can the words *dignity, majesty,* and *holiness* even begin to be appropriate.[21]

The charge of projection now arises anew. What is projected in this notion of Divine Being which, by definition, can never intersect finite experience? Guilt in the wretchedness of humanity? But that is the worst form of anthropomorphism. Traits that exalt the *ground* or *power* of the cosmos by debasing personality? But that is blasphemy. Worship of a Something instead of a Someone? But that is idolatry.

Whatever the motives of the theologian, let every person ask himself: When Jesus says, ". . . I ascend unto my Father, and your Father . . ." (John 20:17) what does He mean? And if there is revulsion at His meaning, does the revulsion come out of reverence based on the revelation of God? Or is it really irreverence based on tradition and guilt which one cannot but project to "God"? The sword of anthropomorphism and psychologism cuts two ways. Which way?[22]

"Things More Noble"

Now let us abandon this mode of analysis and turn to an entirely different question, using the language of the heart.

What is the religious power of this idea? What are its effects as it moves along the threads of the inner life? Let us mark only one of the needs of man and gesture, at least, toward its glowing realization.

There is in all of us an apparently infinite, and certainly, ultimate, need for a rich, abiding, undergirding, trustworthy love. This is a love that reaches in and through the self, outward to others, and upward to the highest in the universe. In

---

21The ordinary layman *does* ignore such theological restrictions because, as Whitehead once said, "Aristotle's God (First Cause)) is not available for religious purposes."

22The psychologist can at most remind us that we often tend to believe what is emotionally satisfying and to disbelieve what is austere and forbidding. What he cannot do is decide, by examining men's psyches, whether their projections really correspond to reality. That can only be settled by examining reality; and if it be said that we cannot know reality, that is simply another (projected?) decision about the nature of reality. For the Mormon the question of God can only be decided by revelation.

the ordinary world, even the world of religion, this craving finds extremely rare fulfillment, though it is talked about ceaselessly. But a dawning understanding is the key to its creative source and the beginning of its increase and transformation: that man was known and loved profoundly even prior to mortal birth; that love, indeed, drew him and his Eternal Father together in a sphere of perfected light and glory; that he, distinct from all other beings, animate or inanimate, in the universe, is a chosen and begotten spirit of the Divine; that this sonship, as well as the "second birth" through Jesus Christ, is at the core of any question about the meaning of life.

Of this sweeping awareness the Prophet Joseph spoke to a multitude of 20,000 enthralled under his voice:

> This is good doctrine. It tastes good. I can taste the principles of eternal life, and so can you. They are given to me by the revelations of Jesus Christ. . . . and when I tell you of these things which were given me by inspiration of the Holy Spirit, you are bound to receive them as sweet, and rejoice more and more.[23]

Man has always believed that somehow God could be in his heart. Now he realizes that godliness is veritably engrained in him through a divine lineage. And the whole of his soul lights up.

A child orphaned and cuffed about in a hostile world craves the lifting power of a person who radiates every cherished aspiration. Now comes the recognition that this is *inspiration,* that a real, living parent is here announcing, arms outstretched, "I am yours! And you are mine!"

A mother and father look down at their sleeping infant, in communing touch with what is sacred to both. Parental love, they see in this illumined moment, is not a shadow but a light of divine love in which splendor we became spirit children and by which we were enveloped.

---

[23]*Teachings of the Prophet Joseph Smith,* page 355. This was the last major address the Prophet delivered in the Nauvoo Grove prior to his death.

These, with a wealth of poignant insights that follow in their wake, reveal meaning in human existence. In relationship to the divine they replace the grosser emotions of fear, distant awe, dread, bitter solitude, and even despair, with the subtler and finer feelings: gratitude, virtue akin to virtue, lightness of spirit, embracing sympathy, peace of soul, and motivation to share. They uncover layer after layer of worldly facade. They electrify, inspire, and ennoble. They are, in truth, the source and power of love.

To the degree that Christendom denies the genuine fatherhood of God and the genuine sonship of man's spirit (and both Christendom and the major world religions do deny them) they have lost the image of man's real origin and therefore the image of his real destiny. They deny the "power of godliness."

All the rapturous things that are said about the love or *agape* of God who sent His Only Begotten in the flesh are hollow when coupled with the dogma that He did *not* so love us that He distinguished us from the rest of creation by implanting in us the potential of His own likeness. The dogma "lessens man." But, as any reference to a contemporary book on theology will show, it also lessens God, even while claiming to dignify Him. Shall we reject the shining truth because it is so shining?

Many of us in the modern world are prodigal sons. We have not only left home, we have forgotten it and the Father who still waits to unfold to us not only "all that I *have*" but also, "all that I *am*."

But only our actual sonship can account for this miracle: that an inner flame apprehends and affirms what the creeds and our own darkened thoughts solemnly deny. This flame is not quickened, but neither is it quenched when, asking for the bread of the living Father, we are given the stone of dead "being-itself."

This is the flame that is rekindled when a Prophet testifies in the 20th century as Jesus Christ did in the first, "God is our Father." An intuitive flash dissipates theological and psychological speculation. A luminous nostalgia arises in us. And as if from a far-off center, the glow of an evanescent past re-awakens responses of awesome love we find it impossible to describe. And that is why, from the millions who listen to the strains of the Mormon Tabernacle Choir annually, a frequent request is for the music and words of a simple Mormon hymn. This is a hymn that expresses the heart of "Latter-day Saint-liness." It is, "O My Father."[24]

---

[24]Of this hymn President Wilford Woodruff said, "That hymn is a revelation, though it was given unto us by a woman, Sister Eliza R. Snow. There are a great many sisters who have the spirit of revelation. There is no reason why they should not be inspired as well as men." *Discourses of Wilford Woodruff*, Book-craft, Salt Lake City, page 62.

The Spirit
and the Body

*Nor hath God designed to show Himself elsewhere
more clearly than in human form sublime; which, since
they image Him, alone I love. (from "Heaven-born
Beauty" — Michelangelo.)*

CHAPTER IV

WE CAME INTO this world that we might receive
a body and present it pure before God in the
celestial kindom.

The great principle of happiness consists in having
a body.

All beings who have bodies have power over those
who have not.[1]

---

[1]*Teachings of the Prophet Joseph Smith*, Joseph Fielding Smith (editor), Deseret News Press, Salt Lake City, Utah, 1938; pages 352, 181.

The Spirit and the Body

One of the all-time bafflements of life is this: Why is man embodied? Has the body a lasting purpose in nature or in the plan of God?

The question and typical answers have been badly blurred, due in great measure to the dogma of immaterialism. This assumption born in Greece now dominates both Judaism and Christianity and infiltrates the thought of the entire Western world.[2] The assumption is that there are two utterly different divisions of reality, one immaterial and the other material. Mind or soul or spirit are immaterial. Body is material.[3]

The dualisms that result tend to become radical: the soul has none of the qualities of the body and vice versa. Mind or soul is really real, the body is unreal or less real. The soul is eternal; the body temporal. The soul is good; the body is evil.[4]

In our time the focus shifts to the dualism of "finite reality" and "infinite reality," or of particular beings and being-itself, or of the objective-experimental and the Transcendent-existential. But in some form the old disjunction remains. And the mortal body is deemed inferior or demonic.

And thus arise a vast array of puzzles. How can two entities that have nothing in common, not even existence in space and time, be conjoined in any sense? How can one influence the other? Why would an unembodied God create an embodied man to achieve a disembodied immortality?

---

[2] For a dualistic approach to eastern religion see Walter T. Stace's *Time and Eternity*, University Press, Princeton, 1952. For a summary of the dualism in Christian thought of our time see *The Search for Meaning in Life*, Robert F. Davidson (editor); Holt, Rinehart and Winston, New York, 1962; Section 5.

[3] The work of St. Thomas and the Scholastics revolved around this issue, with Platonic and Aristotelian premises — the relegating of the "heavenly" to immateriality, (the angels, for example, are "pure species") and of the "earthly" to materiality or corporeality. The "double truth" concept grew in this area as well as the distinction, still basic to Roman Catholic theology, between metaphysics and physics.

[4] The tendency to call the body evil was manifest most sharply in the Manichees and this, in turn, is supposedly derived from Persian dualism. Common distinctions still lead, and mislead, our thought in religion; e.g. sacred vs. secular, spiritual vs. temporal. Modern revelation dissolves the distinction. See Doctrine and Covenants 29:31-35.

In reaction to the dogmas of a "ghost in the machine," modern naturalistic and scientific outlooks take the position of physicalism.[5] Physicalism denies that there is evidence for the shadowy entities, "mind" or "soul," of traditional definition. Whatever the body is, it is all there is. Man is "nothing but" nucleic acids, cell structures, nerve nets, and the complicated phenomena called "mental."[6]

Thus immaterialists try to live as if there were no body, and physicalists try to live as if there were no soul or spirit.[7]

Almost universally today it is assumed that only if immaterialism or Transcendence be defended can God and religion be salvaged, and that if it be rejected both are disposed of. Over this issue major Catholic, Protestant, and Jewish faiths contend with Marxists, humanists, and many natural scientists.

The Elements of Selfhood

Here again Joseph Smith faces a confusing colossus. And with revelatory insight he replaces it. It turns out that deception is on both sides of the controversy. Without full awareness of its philosophical undercurrent, modern man is caught in a riptide. Forced by his environment to favor one side or the other of a traditional "either-or" he rarely recognizes that neither side is a safe guide to the nature of man.

The revolution, which brings a sunburst of self-understanding, is this:

Mind, spirit, and body are all material, in varying degrees of refinement. They have equal status in spatio-temporal existence and are, in their perfected state, of equal worth. Spirit and body are dissimilar enough to require each other in full

---

[5]See, e.g. Alston and Nakhnikian (editors) *Readings in Twentieth Century Philosophy*; Free Press of Glencoe, New York, 1963; parts VII and VIII.

[6]See Gilbert Ryle, *Concept of Mind*; Hutchinson, London, 1949.

[7]It is, of course, impossible to live "as if" there were no body. Yet the view of absolute idealists, Christian Scientists, and certain mystics is that all materiality is illusion. The view tends to quietism, asceticism, and "other-worldliness." Physicalism is a scientific approach and is compatible with various ethical outlooks or ways of life. But typically it leads to hedonism, to an attempt to maximize the natural satisfactions of the body. See Bertrand Russell's *Why I Am Not a Christian*; Simon & Schuster, New York, 1957.

selfhood. But they are similar enough that when our bodies are purified we shall see that "all spirit is matter." Embodied spirits *always* "have an ascendancy" over unembodied spirits.[8]

Thus the immaterialist is wrong in what he affirms (immaterial entities), and the physicalist is wrong in what he denies (spirit entities). And thus a thousand dualistic puzzles and dilemmas collapse.[9]

This is not, as some may suppose, just an issue of word usage. It leads to a revision of attitudes and aspirations that affect the very breath of mankind. To illustrate, here is a cross-sectional comparison of the Prophet's teaching and dominant alternatives.

Immaterialists, e.g. Plotinus, Thomas, Calvin, teach that man was created in a body to prepare for a nontemporal eternity. The Prophet taught that we are living in a temporal eternity. Our co-eternal intelligences were first given spirit bodies and now, as a climax of our development, physical bodies which will have permanence in the resurrection.

Physicalists, e.g. Ryle, Morris, Lamont, teach that there is no "spirit" in combination with body. The body, including its so-called personality traits, reduces to physical genes.[10] The Prophet taught that the spirit-personality was developed long before our physical embodiment and profoundly affects it and that there are real and unmistakable spirit needs as there are body needs.[11]

Extreme immaterialists, e.g. mystics like St. John of the Cross and ascetics like Ghandi, despise "body, parts, and pas-

---

[8]The word "ascendancy" is the Prophet's. He taught repeatedly that it is punishment to be denied a body. See *Teachings of the Prophet Joseph Smith;* pages 297, 306, 312.

[9]The mind-body problem and a variety of solutions is sketched in Albury Castell's *An Introduction to Modern Philosophy;* Macmillan Company, New York, 1953; topic 2.

[10]The Prophet taught that the spiritual creation preceded and was in the likeness of the physical creation. See the Pearl of Great Price, Moses 3:5; and Doctrine and Covenants 77:2; 131:7, 8.

[11]See *Teachings of the Prophet Joseph Smith,* pages 255, 381, 296, 297.

sions" and define God as lacking them.[12] They tend not only to disparage the body but to torment and renounce it. Extreme physicalists, on the other hand (e.g. Russell), teach that since the body is all, it is the sole source of happiness. They tend to define happiness without regard for quality, at least without spiritual modes.[13] A pig satisfied at the trough is better than a Socrates unsatisfied at the trial.

Joseph Smith taught that man's body is the marvelously perfectible instrument of his likewise perfectible mind and spirit. "That which is without body, parts and passions is nothing."[14] There are levels of consciousness, powers of expression, ways of fulfillment in thought, feeling, and action that come only when the threefold nature of man is harmoniously combined.[15] To cultivate the soul is to cultivate both body and spirit.[16]

Nietzsche, speaking for physicalists, maintains that "we are what we eat" and that the body has a total "turnover" every seven years.[17] The Prophet taught that our identity is not simply a thread of memory or a bundle of impressions. None of the eternal elements of our person (even during the temporary disorganization of the body) becomes an essential part of another body.[18]

Boehme, speaking for immaterialists, teaches that our mental and spiritual powers and our communion with God are im-

---

12See St. John of the Cross, Poems (Introduction by M. C. D'Arcy) in Penguin Classics, Baltimore, 1960. See also Ghandi's Autobiography, Washington Public Affairs Press, Washington, 1960.

13The controversy of "quantitative vs. qualitative hedonism" carries over into religion under different labels. The issue is this: are there satisfactions of the self that are more intensive and inclusive as one approaches the likeness of God? And do thy involve withdrawal from the senses? The Prophet answered "yes" to the first question and "no" to the second.

14Teachings of the Prophet Joseph Smith, page 181.

15This point is put in a near-classic form by Parley P. Pratt who, after conversion to Mormonism, wrote an essay (almost unknown to our generation) entitled, "Intelligence and Affection." See Parker Robison (editor), Writings of Parley P. Pratt.

16Indeed the Prophet records in Doctrine and Covenants 93 that the "spirit and the body are the soul of man." The soul of man is the whole of man.

17See Nietzsche, Modern Library Giant; Random House, New York.

18This statement was made in response to a question by Orson Pratt. Recent biology suggests that it is almost as if our own "identification tag" is on each constituent cell of our bodies.

paired by the body.[19] The Prophet taught that our mental and
spiritual powers will ultimately be enhanced by the body. Thus:

> And if your eye be single to my glory, your whole
> bodies shall be filled with light, and there shall be no
> darkness in you; and that body which is filled with light
> comprehendeth all things. (Doctrine and Covenants
> 88:67.)

Immaterialists tend to believe that the body is the product
of sin or error. (In the Orient it is the evil aftermath of
"Karma.") Flesh is utterly depraved, and man's ills began with
the body and will end with it.[20] Some, like Buddha, long for
annihilation.[21]

The Prophet taught that the body is the product of righteousness. We will look upon the temporary absence of our
spirits from our bodies as bondage, not as freedom. (See Doctrine and Covenants 45:17.) "Even here," he taught, "we may
begin to enjoy that which shall be in full hereafter."[22] But only
when the spirit and body are "inseparably connected" or resurrected, in a celestial condition, will we receive a fullness of
glory and thus a fullness of joy. (See Doctrine and Covenants
84, 88, 93.)

Of the Fallen and the Failing

What is good and what is evil about the body?

The three modes of man's makeup, the Prophet taught, are
related so intimately that they delimit or exalt each other together. One cannot say to the other, "I have no need of thee."

19See Jacob Boehme, *Personal Christianity*; Atlantic Paperbacks, Ungar Publishing House, New York. "That which is of the earth and must return to it is
not merely the visible physical body, but also the carnal mind and the astral man
with his earthly desires. There is nothing immortal in man, except that which
is divine in him." Like-minded writers deny that there can be anything divine
about the physical. (page 265.)

20See *Meister Eckhart*, (Raymond B. Blakney, trans.); Harper Torchbook, New
York, 1957. Compare F. C. Happold's *Mysticism*; Pelican Books, Baltimore, Mary-
land, 1963; chapter 24, the "Coinherence of Spirit and Matter."

21"Nirvana" is thought by Western Minds to be a kind of heaven. But many
Oriental writers speak of absolute extinction and certainly mean the loss of all
consciousness.

22*Teachings of the Prophet Joseph Smith*, page 296.

There is not just parallelism but interaction and fusion through the life-giving power of Jesus the Christ.

Is the failure to complete one's nature an evil? Then mind and spirit may be evil as well as the body. Is refinement in knowledge, power, and glory a good? Then the body may be good as well as mind and spirit. In this sense heaven is as secular as earth and the body as sacred as the spirit.

But is not mortal man "fallen" and "carnal, sensual, devilish"?[23] Did not the ancient apostle say to "crucify the flesh with its affections and lusts"?[24] Yes and yes.

But the way of sanctification is *in* the body not *out* of it. And to a marked degree the effects of the purifying process or "new birth" are visible. The inspired way of Christ is not utter renunciation but regeneration, not emasculation but inspired expression, not the way of death but the way of life, not to nurture the poisons of corruption but to replace them with the powers of godliness.

> The nearer a man approaches perfection the clearer are his views and the greater his enjoyments till he has overcome the evils of his life and lost every desire for sin.[25]

The joy that accompanies wholeness is a rich and inclusive joy, of a quality that resounds through the total being. Thus, for Joseph Smith, even the processes of purification are life-giving. They are not, as ironically named, "mortifying." One meaning of fasting and prayer, for example, is "rejoicing and prayer." (See Doctrine and Covenants 59.) The body is sensi-

---

23The Prophet taught that man was fallen and in need of the "second birth." But he did not teach "total depravity"; he did not teach "original sin" if that means *we* participated in Adam's fall metaphysically or symbolically; he did not teach that corporeality was a curse. Man may be not only unfulfilled; but a rebel, shot through with tendencies that lead to further corruption. But the degenerate can become regenerate. For Joseph Smith the problem is worse (it includes mind and spirit in the fall) and regeneration better (it leads to a condition exactly akin to that of the Divine), than traditional views.

24See Paul in Galatians 6. Paul has been credited (or blamed) with a flesh-spirit dualism. But this is a moot question. He clearly saw the difference between corrupt flesh and godly flesh. But he did not teach a doctrine of escape.

25*Teachings of the Prophet Joseph Smith*, page 51.

tized to deeper awareness of the subtler realities of God and
His Spirit. But the experience of rejoicing includes, as it were,
the sense-spectrums of both spirit and body.

The Price of Anguish

Today an avalanche of case books on psychotherapy chron-
icles the miseries of what Menninger calls "Man Against Himself."[26] There are pathetic victims, worshipping in vain one or
the other of the two omnipresent gods, immaterialism and
physicalism. In anguish millions still refuse to believe that negation is futile, dissipation is futile, and escape is impossible.

The attitudes surrounding these religions distill like plasma
into the veins of all of us. It is no surprise that Gabriel Marcel
says with horror, "I am my body,"[27] and that we walk the
streets aware of the body's degenerate dirge unbelieving that
anyone really achieves its transformed symphony.

Psychologists, committed only to the superiority of sanity,
go on telling us that we must learn to "live with ourselves,"some
times in radical disagreement as to the nature of self. They
have the almost desperate hope that there *is* something meaningful, wholesome, spiritual, sublime about the body at its best,
and that somehow self-unity is within reach. (We can vision
this when a lovely being shines through the face of a child,
when what the Prophet called his "glory, bloom, and beauty"
is vividly forecast.)[28] But how long can we hold to this when
our pulse thunders with opposite ideals — that the flesh is a
"nasty, brutish" shack, or that it is a supersensual castle? Where
in heaven or earth is the power to make the body what an
ancient disciple of Christ said it was: a living Temple of the
Spirit of God?

This *is* the Truth and Power re-revealed through the
Prophet Joseph Smith. And it is the restoration of wholeness.

26See Menninger and Hillner (editors), *Constructive Aspects of Anxiety*; Ab-
ingdon Press, New York, 1963.

27See Marcel on the "limit situation" the body imposes in John Wild, *The
Challenge of Existentialism*; Bloomington, Indiana, 1955.

28Speaking of the resurrection, the Prophet says "they glory in bloom and
beauty. No man can describe it to you, no man can write it." *Teachings of the
Prophet Joseph Smith*, page 368.

Modern man is not imprisoned in his body but imprisoned in a set of distortions of it. Man, not God, has turned his body into a perpetual torture chamber.

The feeling truth is that the body is the crowning stage of progressive unfoldment toward celestial personality.

The redeeming truth is that Jesus Christ lived and died not only to heal, lift, and fulfill all men but *all of man* — intelligence, spirit, and body. And He exemplified magnificently the possible final outcome.

The glorifying truth is that the transformation of the Spirit of God that emanates through Christ in His perfected condition reaches to the very cell structure and bloodstream, to the very affections and tendencies of our composite nature. The only lasting sorrow will be in the measure we fail to receive the power of His promise: that some day we may be fashioned like unto Him!

This philosophy of embodiment is destined not only to conquer the world, but to redeem and sanctify it under the feet of radiant sons and daughters of God. These, in the likeness of God and through the power of Christ, will be embodied light and enlightened bodies — forever.

Evil and Suffering

. . . Know thou, my son, that all these things shall give thee experience, and shall be for thy good.

The Son of Man hath descended below them all. Art thou greater than he?[1]

CHAPTER V

THE MOST STAGGERING objection to belief in a personal God is the ugly, tragic, overwhelming fact of human inequality and suffering.

Dare we uncover this stark reality, not as an academic toy, but at its worst?

As a beginning, let us walk into a hospital.

---

[1]Doctrine and Covenants 122:7, 8. These words were received and written after the Prophet had languished four months in the darkness of Liberty Jail.

Here. This newborn infant with the lovely face. She could not have had worthier parents. But she was born in total paralysis and is blind. The doctors do not know whether she will survive. And if she does. . . .

This bed is empty. Its occupant, a quivering psychotic with a wild stare, is upstairs undergoing shock treatment. He collapsed when his wife and two children were maimed in a fire, one beyond recognition.

Over here is a surgeon who had a rare brain disease and asked his closest friend to operate. The operation failed; and he has been, for nearly three years, a human vegetable. His friend has since committed suicide.

Somewhere tonight the families of these souls are crying themselves to sleep.

Now, if your arm will hold out, write as many zeros after a "1" as will portray similar reenactments of these scenes that are, or have been, or may be, on this planet. And that will be one thread in the tapestry of human misery.

Come next to the roof of the hospital and gaze up at the order and design of the stars. Do they prove that God is there? What, then, is proved by the utter disorder, the cruel indifference, the fantastic meaninglessness of life below us? Does God care more about the stars than about His children?

Traditionally, the last resort (if not the first) of the believer in God, under this twisting knife, is: "Strange and inscrutable are the ways of the Divine."

But this retreat to mystery, even for its advocates, leaves gnawing anxieties. So have arisen two major efforts at reconciliation. One approach says that evil is not really real. It is privative, or perspectival, or illusory.[2] The other approach says that evil *is* really real, worse, even, than the enemies of religion

---

[2]That evil is "privation," absence of good, not a positive reality, is the official view of Roman Catholicism. That evil is in our "perspective" but disappears under the eternal perspective is the view of Leibniz, Spinoza and Josiah Royce. That evil is illusory is the view of Christian Science, Buddhism, and some forms of spiritualism.

have said.[3] The one supposes to exonerate God by denying evil. The other supposes strangely to placate man by exaggerating it. The one says there is no problem, the other implies that there is no hope. Both are mistaken.

Let us summon, now, a prophet-son of modern times.

We will require that he know, in the very marrow of his bones, the excruciating anguish of mortal life.[4] For nothing is more barren, to one in agony, than pat answers which seem the unfeeling evasions of a distant spectator who "never felt a wound."

Let us introduce the Prophet Joseph Smith to the mother of a blind baby. Listen to the queries of her heart in this imaginary dialogue.[5] And mark how these, the merest kernels of his prophetic grasp of man's origins, radically alter typical reflections on suffering.[6]

MOTHER: Is what I am going through "illusion"? Is it "all in my mind"?

THE PROPHET: Suffering often results from illusions. But whether or not we face reality as it is, suffering is still real and none escape it. Christ did not.

MOTHER: But why did not God prevent what has happened to me? Why should I or my child be the victims? What have we done to deserve this?

THE PROPHET: You assume suffering is always a form of Divine punishment. It is not. You are convinced by Job's "friends" instead of by Job.[7] But let us go further back. It is true

---

[3]This is the approach of "crisis theology" and existentialism. Instead of minimizing evil their ruthless portrayal of its modes maximizes it. So desperate is the plight of man that futility dominates. Religion reduces to stoical endurance and/or despair.

[4]Rarely, if ever, has so much of relentless trial and soul struggle been crowded into one life as in Joseph Smith's.

[5]The dialogue is imaginary, but the ideas are not. The "Mother" poses questions that have been raised numberless times. For every sentence in the Prophet's "replies" there is a first-hand counterpart in his writings or sermons.

[6]This is only an outline of the Prophet's teachings, some ways in which the backward look to premortal life affects the question.

[7]See the 38th chapter of Job where, the Prophet taught, there is a display of the human tendency to conclude that suffering is always the wrath of an angry God. This is an "unhallowed principle." See *Teachings of the Prophet Joseph Smith*, edited by Joseph Fielding Smith, Deseret News Press, Salt Lake City, Utah, 1938, page 162.

that God can prevent (as He can induce) some kinds of suffering. But not all.[8]

MOTHER: What do you mean? Is not God all powerful? Are not all things possible with Him? How can we have faith in a limited God?

THE PROPHET: The question is rather how we can have faith in the "unconditioned" God of the Creeds. The Creeds say that God, being Absolute in power, could have created the universe and its creatures in a utopia of happiness and without pain. They say that with Absolute foreknowledge our "freedom" would be hopelessly abused. He elected not to return this mass of humanity to nothing, but to thrust it into a worse, and endless, torment.[9]

Non-Christians call such a God "monstrous." Many Christians call Him (or "It") "inscrutable" and live, for all their talk of love, in terror. Thank God the living God has revealed that no such god exists.

MOTHER: But if God is not behind all our suffering, what is? Are you saying there is some other ultimate explanation?

THE PROPHET: Yes. You have been taught that God is the total cause of everything. The truth is that He is not the *total* cause of anything.[10]

MOTHER: What, then?

THE PROPHET: God is forever surrounded by us, by co-eternal intelligences, and by the self-existent elements and principles of reality. These are as unoriginated as He is.

Now the Creeds say that God has always been God. But this well-motivated expression of reverence is a solemn travesty. The truth is infinitely more inspiring: that God

---

[8]If, for example, evil be defined as delimitation in growth, conflict of wills, refusal to receive the love and power of God, seeking to become a law unto oneself, then evil is eternal. For always there will be intelligences, spirits, and resurrected beings in these conditions.

[9]See Henry D. Aiken's latest treatment of the classic argument that evil proves God does not exist: "God and Evil" in *Reason and Conduct*; Alfred A. Knopf, New York, 1962.

[10]See *Teachings of the Prophet Joseph Smith*, pages 158, 181, 350, 351, 354.

Himself *became* God (whose power now extends in and through all things) by the mastery of the same ultimate and unchanging conditions to which you and I are subject. So, likewise, did His Firstborn Son, Jesus the Christ.[11]

In His relationship to us, "all things are possible" that are possible. But some things are impossible. We cannot have crucial experience without having it. We cannot unfold into His fulness except in His way. We cannot develop without stress nor be perfected without suffering. The belief that we can write "God" in front of these statements and thus remove the "nots" is an illusion that will only end in disillusion.[12]

MOTHER: But why do some suffer so much more than others? Are we not created equal?

THE PROPHET: We are equal as far as the concern, and the pure, glorious, fatherly love of God are concerned; for we are all spiritually begotten of Him. And no superlative in our present language can describe this love. We are also equal before the law, eternal law.

But in our original natures we are *un*created and *un*equal. Individual differences (and therefore needs) predate mortality and even our beginnings as spirits. They are "gnolaum" or eternal![13] God did not create them so. Thus, no waving of a Divine wand can transform a Satan into a Christ nor a Christ into a Satan. In nobility, and in response to the sanctifying powers that emanate from God the

---

[11]See the "King Follett Discourse," and footnotes by B. H. Roberts, *Ibid.*, page 342. The rare notion that God is in a sense finite, limited by the nature of His environment, has been taught in some form by such men as William James, A. N. Whitehead, Charles Hartshorne, E. S. Brightman, and A. C. Garnett. See also *Twentieth Century Religious Thought*, Harper and Row, New York, 1963; Chapter XVII.

[12]Traditional theology has taught that God's "all-powerfulness" is limited only by the laws of contradiction. Yet, theologians continue to maintain that it is impossible for God, being infinite, to manifest Himself to man in literal revelation, and likewise impossible for God to transform man into His literal likeness. It turns out, therefore, that in these and other ways, the living God of modern revelation is *more* powerful than the "god" of the classical creeds.

[13]See Pearl of Great Price, Abraham 3:18, 19, 22, 23. See also B. H. Roberts, *Seventys' Year Book*, Volume IV; Skelton Publishing Company, Salt Lake City, Utah, 1912; Lesson IV.

Father, they differ. And so do all the spirit sons and daughters of God.

MOTHER: But what has this to do with me? Why has God thrown us into this world with these horrible handicaps? Why? Why?

THE PROPHET: Again, you assume that God alone accounts for your being here and that handicaps are all necessarily final and horrible. Instead, you and the child of your bosom counseled intimately with God the Father. Freely, fully, and with a courage that astonishes mortal imagination, you elected and prepared for this estate. The contrasts of the flesh, its risks, its terrific trials were known to you. More than that, you comprehended your actual appointed mission in this world, designed to meet your individual needs, and those who would depend upon you. Perhaps you anticipated these exact circumstances.[14]

Why did you make an irrevocable covenant to enter the flesh? You recognized that, whatever the price, the increasing glory, light, and power of the Divine was in every way worth it!

MOTHER: But that seems so cruel. Did not Christ come to relieve suffering? Are not His disciples to be blessed?

THE PROPHET: Christ came that suffering might result not only in good, but in its perfect work, which is perfection. He did not live to end all suffering, but to end all needless suffering and to turn suffering into joy, even in this world.[15]

Let me explain.

14"The organization of the spiritual and heavenly worlds, and of spiritual and heavenly beings, was agreeable to the most perfect order and harmony: their limits and bounds were fixed irrevocably, and voluntarily subscribed to in their heavenly estate by themselves, and were by our first parents subscribed to upon the earth. Hence the importance of embracing and subscribing to principles of eternal truth by all men upon the earth that expect eternal life." *Teachings of the Prophet Joseph Smith,* page 325.

15Latter-day Saints tend to ignore the context of the oft-quoted passage of Lehi's: ". . . Men are, that they might have joy." (2 Nephi 2:25.) Lehi teaches that joy could not arise except through contrasts of mortality. Mortal life is sweet, but it is bittersweet.

In our own inner experience we can trace the opposite products of pain. At this hour life seems blinding, devastating. Yet it is a measure of our discipleship of Christ that even sorely grievous hours have yielded enlightenment, a budding knowledge of self and others, and ennoblement. When we search ourselves, it is no mystery that good, the purifying force of godliness, may arise out of affliction. (Looking back we may wonder whether anything we really prize comes without it.)

This should caution us in judging what is and what is not a blessing in this life.

MOTHER: Yes. I recognize that precious things of mind and spirit cannot come from ease, nor from evasion of struggle. But such suffering as this, so meaningless, so destructive, often leads to worse suffering, and that, in turn, to worse. Why so vast a sum in the world?

THE PROPHET: We are on the threshold now of a sum you may rarely have contemplated. The premortal relationship we had with Jesus Christ was a prevision of our descent and ascent.[16] Then, as now, we shrank from innocent suffering. For this is of the essence of love.

But what is left to the Tender Parent who *cannot* (not simply, *will not*) force His spirit-child into the path of self-realization? What lifting power exceeds all others in our stages of deficiency, ignorance, and then a corrupt nature?[17] It is the completely voluntary, and completely undeserved, suffering of "the Lamb slain from before the foundation of the world." Somehow that is infinite. The innate mercy of

---

16"The Father called all spirits before Him at the creation of man, and organized them." "At the first organization in heaven we were all present, and saw the Saviour chosen and appointed and the plan of salvation made, and we sanctioned it." *Teachings of the Prophet Joseph Smith,* pages 158, 181.

17C. S. Lewis argues in his *Problem of Pain,* New York, Macmillan Company, 1962, that God is Omnipotent, yet insists that God *cannot* make us susceptible to His grace without pain, and adds that some are incapable even then. The Prophet taught that experience itself is invaluable, and that our individual callings involve suffering in the service of humanity. The widest experience in trial is the most desirable. (See Roberts' comment on "Sweet are the uses of adversity," *The Gospel,* Deseret Book Company, Salt Lake City, 1950; page 290.)

our spirits was heightened in the presence of His compassion.[18] And in this world, often through pain, we are re-awakened in our spirit to the Christ who really was and is. Only the most darkened soul can flout the profound inner craving that His suffering, and all else, even the tremors of your infant, may yield power and purity, and not finally be in vain.

MOTHER: Was His sacrifice necessary to enable us to rise into a life like His?

THE PROPHET: Yes. But the warm and overwhelming miracle is this: the more we approach Him and His likeness, the more we come to love as He loves, and the less we suffer needlessly.[19]

These physical losses and tribulations, if endured in His name, have their limits and are refining. The apparently, but not really, limitless mental and spiritual anguish that arises from life's buffetings takes on meaning. Pain becomes a laboratory of soul-nurture, and we may "count it all joy." The darkest abyss has its own revelations, its own chrysalis of higher promise. This is not myth! I testify it is the deepest secret of life.

MOTHER: It is all so hard, so hard.

THE PROPHET: Yes. Yet strangely beautiful. In your present nightmare a voice whips you with *why,* and *if only,* and *how long,* and *what might have been.* All that I have said may seem empty. But that fever will pass.

18"For intelligence cleaveth unto intelligence; wisdom receiveth wisdom; truth embraceth truth; virtue loveth virtue; light cleaveth unto light; mercy hath compassion on mercy and claimeth her own . . ." (Doctrine and Covenants 88:40.)

19We need not suffer further for our sinfulness, for through Him we may be redeemed. We need not suffer further from false expectations, for as we increase in righteousness, His revelations replace error with truth. Eventually, we need not suffer in the threat of final failure and condemnation. For as we prove that we are "determined to serve the Lord at all hazards" we can receive the assurance of eternal life, "an anchor to the soul, sure and steadfast." "Though the thunders might roll and lightnings flash, and earthquakes bellow, and war gather thick around, yet this hope and knowledge would support the soul in every hour of trial, trouble and tribulation. Then knowledge through our Lord and Saviour Jesus Christ is the grand key that unlocks the glories and mysteries of the kingdom of heaven." *Teachings of the Prophet Joseph Smith,* page 298.

And as it does, you will be newly sensitive to the flashes of revelation that are your privilege in the quiet soundings of your soul. They alone can give you individual testimony of this hour's actual meaning for you. They alone can convincingly witness what seems now so utterly unbelievable. You are in the very hollow of the hand of God, a hand that will not, by your premortal request, remove you from the furnace; but will see you through it.[20]

Whatever the Lord's individual word to you may be, there are two abiding certainties.

The awful tragedy of this life, as of the next, is not suffering. It is "suffering in vain." Or worse, it is suffering that could have been the elixir of nobility, transforming us into a godliness beyond description which, instead, has become the poison of bitterness and alienation.[21]

But this is equally certain: from the smoldering rubble of our lives, stricken and agonized though they be, there can arise, through Christ, an incredible shining joy, a joy in the image of Christ who is the image of God who overcame all things.

"All your losses will be made up to you in the resurrection provided you continue faithful. By the vision of the Almighty I have seen it."[22] For you, your child, as for the Father and Christ, there was, there is no other way.

20"I assure the Saints that truth, in reference to these matters, can and may be known through the revelations of God in the way of His ordinances, and in answer to prayer." Ibid., page 325.

21The Prophet was counseled in his youth, "Be patient in afflictions for thou shalt have many." (Doctrine and Covenants 24:8.) "If I obtain the glory which I have in view, I expect to wade through much tribulation." (Juvenile Instructor, Volume 27, page 173.) And toward the end he said, "Every wave of adversity has only wafted me that much closer to Deity." Brigham Young observed that the Prophet was more perfected in 38 years with severe trials than he could have been in a thousand years without them.

22Teachings of the Prophet Joseph Smith, page 296.

Freedom
and Fulfillment

All is voluntary. . . . God will not exert any compulsory means and the Devil cannot.[1]

CHAPTER VI

ANY APPROACH to the nature of man leads to the question of freedom. In what sense, if at all, is man free?

Paradoxically, this is a question we are not free to ignore. We agonize over it daily. The impact of life upon us, or, if we prefer, our impact on life compels us to ask ourselves — What is "within my power" and what is not? Did I have to happen? Does anything or everything have to happen? Given the same conditions could I have been or done otherwise?

---

[1] *Teachings of the Prophet Joseph Smith*, page 187.

The central issue, put loosely, is whether or not man can upset the causal chain? The determinist answers, "No." The indeterminist answers, "Yes."[1] In our time there is a certain freshness to the stalemate as three developments have given birth to new searches and researches.

1. *On the side of determinism.*

Some forms of psychology and psychoanalysis point to the immense domination of man's subconscious which, in turn, is fueled by traceable stimuli. These, apparently, are in no way separable from prior causation. Hypnotized, to illustrate, a person may be told that on awakening he will take off his shirt and stand on his head, but that he will forget the instruction. He does so, then invents the most ingenious but clearly false "reasons" for his behavior. Question: Is not all our conduct thus controlled and is not "freedom" just a name for our ignorance of hidden causes?[2]

2. *On the side of indeterminism.*

The so-called Heisenberg principle in quantum physics affirms that inanimate particles at the sub-atomic level behave in unpredictable ways. Neither their position nor velocity can be charted accurately. Explanation, therefore, must be statistical. By analogy, we can predict the approximate number, but not the exact identity, of persons who will be killed or injured on a Labor Day weekend. The logic of the point, at least for Eddington and Born, is that being indeterminate, the particles are therefore undetermined, therefore "free."[3] Question: If

---

[1] Some sentence definitions: The determinist says all events are caused. The indeterminist says some events, namely acts of free will, are uncaused. The fatalist says some or all events are predetermined or "fated" by forces beyond man. The predestinarian says that man's salvation, and/or damnation, was unconditionally decided by God's from eternity. The behaviorist says all behavior is due to man's reaction with environment. The mechanist says the world, and man, are machines moving like a computer. Mormonism fits in none of these pigeon-holes. (See Note 9.) (See for a discussion of the controversy: *Free Will,* Morgenbesser and Walsh (eds.); Englewood Cliffs, N. J., Prentice-Hall, Spectrum Books, 1962.)

[2] See discussion on this issue in *Readings in Ethical Theory,* Hospers and Sellars (eds.); New York, Appleton, 1952; Section, "Guilt and Responsibility."

[3] See Arthur S. Eddington, *Nature of the Physical World,* Cambridge University Press, 1953. An answer to this argument from the point of view of a determinist is in *Determinism and Freedom in the Age of Modern Science,* ed. by Sidney Hook; New York, Collier Books, 1961; "The Case for Determinism," by Brand Blanshard, pages 19-30.

inanimate matter behaves "freely," why reject the belief that man does?

3. Then there is existential analysis.

Writers on man's depth awareness, from Nietzsche to Sartre, from Berdyaev to Heidegger, find freedom an invincible datum in our inner consciousness. They uncover an inferno of guilt toward the past — what I might have done; another inferno of anxiety (not just suspense) toward the future — what I might yet be. In dramatic ways they show that no one, not even the most hardheaded determinist, is able to relieve himself of the sense of personal, and admittedly dreadful, freedom. If we could really believe in a thoroughgoing way that what we are and do is unavoidable, we could not consistently feel guilt for we could not sincerely feel responsible. Question: Why not acknowledge on the surface what we all profoundly encounter in the depths?[4]

In the Beginning

In classical and contemporary debate, one supposition passes unquestioned. Determinists and indeterminists alike suppose that man had a beginning over which he had no control. There are different versions, e.g. "First Cause," "Nature," "Chance," and "God." But, in any case, the view maintains that self-awareness and freedom, whatever they are, came with or after this creation.

Modern revelation not only undercuts this assumption but in an all-important way reverses it. To say that "Man was also in the beginning *with* God," and that "All intelligence is independent in that sphere in which God has placed it to act for itself," is to say that man never has been totally a product.[5]

4For a contrast of the scientific and existential approaches to freedom see my article, "The Contribution of Existentialism," *BYU Studies*, Vol. I, No. 1, Winter, 1959.

5Doctrine and Covenants 93:29. Compare the Prophet's statement, "Intelligence is eternal and exists upon a self-existing principle. It is a spirit from age to age and there is no creation about it." *Teachings of the Prophet Joseph Smith,* edited by Joseph Fielding Smith; Deseret News Press, Salt Lake City, Utah, 1958; page 354.

His uncreated intelligence is active and self-propelling.[6] The process of generation and combination of elements that developed spirit and physical bodies followed, instead of preceding, his independent existence.[7] In this sense man is an eternal co-cause through all stages and all sequences of existence.

Man's Destiny

But with this doctrine of freedom is a doctrine of destiny. Man's nature includes not only the innate possibilities of prime intelligence, but also the embryonic nature of his Eternal Father. In the unfolding process he has already made decisions that are irrevocable and eternal in scope. These, with an everlasting environment, condition him. And from these conditions there is no retreat.[8]

To outline the extensive philosophical implications of this view and its bearing on a hornet's nest of puzzles is impossible here.[9] I turn instead to a close look at some of our everyday reflections on freedom. For when these views are accepted as true, some of our most common and cherished notions are immediately revised.

What Is Freedom?

We ordinarily define and defend freedom as the yearning to breathe free, free from pushy parents, blustery policemen,

---

[6]This, at least, was the Prophet's understanding of uncreate intelligence. See the relevant quotations and comments of B. H. Roberts in the *Seventy's Year Book*, Volume 4, The Atonement, Lessons I and II. Roberts concludes from scriptural statements, and the later discourses of the Prophet, that reason, imagination, and volition are among the innate qualities of intelligence.

[7]The view that freedom is only explicable if we assume man's premortal existence is defended by John Wisdom in *Philosophy and Psycho Analysis*; Oxford, Blackwell, 1953. The difficulties of reconciling the evidence both for causation and freedom are outlined in *Foundations of Ethics*, W. D. Ross; Oxford, Clarendon Press, 1939; chapter, "Determinism and Indeterminism."

[8]The decision to enter mortality in a physical body, for example, is final. Not just in the sense that consequences will extend forever. But in the sense that the embodied condition will be everlasting.

[9]There are puzzles, for example, such as Augustine's — what God was doing before He created man and how man can be blameworthy for acts which follow inevitably from the nature which God created. Another is how the indeterminist can establish responsibility when he says that "free will" events "just happen."

The "Gordian knot" is cut not by indeterminism, but by *self-determination*. Cause-effect relationships, apparently, are universal. But man is, and always has been, one of the unmoved movers, one of the originating causes in the network.

the fetters of red tape, etc. We are so defensive that often we refuse to do what we had decided to do when someone tells us that we "must" do it. (The suspicion may haunt us that we are not really upholding our freedom but exhibiting our slavery to pride.) Many have died for the "four freedoms," for rights of "freedom from." But more precious still is "freedom for," freedom for turning external pressures into internal gains, freedom for becoming what we have it in us to become, the emergence of our authentic selves. Such freedom can flourish or flounder independent of the "inalienable rights." It is the kind of liberty Joseph Smith could not be denied, even in the darkened squalor of Liberty Jail.[10]

Freedom and Law

We talk as if freedom were opposed to law when we say, "There ought to be a law against that"; or when we speak in timid lament about "the long right arm of the law."

But whatever may be said of the laws of men, in the eternal scheme, law is the guarantor of freedom. The continuities of our existence, the exceptionless conditions of life, give freedom its lasting power. If, when we flip a coin, it can be both (or neither) heads or tails, if *anything* can really happen following any action, then the freedom of both coins and men is meaningless. The power of man's agency, because of the greater power of God's, can turn the "bounds and conditions" of action into good. And when we seek to become "a law unto ourselves," we are not masters of law, but victims of it, forced to remain unfulfilled.[11] We do not chortle about "getting away with murder" when we recognize that what we are killing is our own potential.

10See *Man's Search for Meaning*, Viktor E. Frankl; New York, Washington Square Press; pages 206-210. Frankl survived two years in the most incredibly loathsome conditions in the death camps of Auschwitz. His approach to freedom is unusual on the present scene.

11There are, to every kingdom, certain "bounds and conditions." All beings who "abide not" those conditions are not justified. Law enables us to be perfected and sanctified. Doctrine and Covenants 88:34-61; 130:20, 21.

Freedom and Responsibility Are Brothers

We talk as if freedom is incompatible with foreknowledge, as when we say of a spontaneous act that it was "just on impulse" or "just for the dickens of it." But is it not apparent that the fullest exercise of freedom requires foreknowledge, knowledge of our actual possibilities, of reachable ends and effective means? Lacking it, we are at best moles in a maze in pointless quest of survival, for what? The disillusion of our time is largely the effect of lost moorings and the terrible suspense of the unforeseen. "Men's hearts fail them" thus. And hence arise a dozen forms of fatalism invoked because it is apparently more bearable to believe the future is all fixed, than to believe it still depends — on us. Thus religions of grace-alone and psychologies of adjustment-alone perpetuate imprisonment. They encourage us to accept our soul-sicknesses in the conviction that there is nothing we can do.[12]

We often recite glibly the chain of blame, making excuses in a way that does not separate the sheep from the scapegoats. Everyone can blame everyone else, who, happily, can blame others still. Even the devil comes in for his undue share.[13] But the logic, or rather psychologic, of the position is that since the devil shows signs of being a compulsive sadist he should not be held responsible, certainly not punished. He no doubt had delinquent parents!

The truth is that any chain-tracing will eventually lead us to ourselves, and some sovereign decision. Addictions of character, for example, may justify the cry, "I can't help it." But it can always be said truly, "You could have helped it."

---

[12]Indeed, some writers on freedom are convinced that most doctrines of causal necessity have been invented subjectively by men to cover up their needling sense of responsibility. Determinism is an intellectual tranquilizer. But William James says lucidly why another part of us finds determinism intolerable, though he does not prove the existence of free will. See his essay, "Dilemma of Determinism," available in many paperback collections.

[13]"There are three independent principles: the spirit of God, the spirit of man, and the spirit of the devil. All men have power to resist the devil." *Teachings of the Prophet Joseph Smith*, page 189.

We Are Free to Change

On the other hand we talk at times as if freedom were a constant, available whenever we want to use it. "I could do it (or stop doing it) if I wanted to." When praise is in order, it is customary to claim to be "self-made," as if, for example, according to our own fancy, we can live without breathing and breathe without air.

Actually, the most frightening power of freedom is to freely give itself up to forces that stunt it. An acorn can become an oak or less than an oak, but not something else. So with us. In an acorn there are indispensable elements of nurture. So with us. Unlike the acorn, we have intelligent initiative that can go astray. In this realm the role of Christ is to break the bonds of our diminishing freedom and reenthrone our becoming. In crucial ways only He can do this.[14] But here again, He *cannot* if we *will* not. We must will and seek and apply His powers with the measure of control that remains to us. The measure is always more than zero. "There is never a time when the spirit is too old to approach God."[15]

Freedom Involves Commitment

We talk as if freedom consisted in having the greatest variety of options and that a "once-and-for-all" decision coerces our initiative. But is freedom increased by every new flavor of ice cream?

Actually, it is only when we rise above trivial options and ask ourselves in the depths, "What do I want *to be*?" that we emerge from the bondage of a flitting and faceless mode of life.[16] The most majestic wonder of our freedom is that we can

---

14This is the true version of predestination, namely, that the *means* of our redemption were predetermined in harmony with eternal law and as sanctioned voluntarily by us. But our own agency was not "predetermined" except as its exercise carries over into our present tendencies. "God did predestinate that all who were saved would be saved through Jesus Christ, but *unconditional* election was not taught by the ancient apostles." *Ibid.*, page 189.

15*Ibid.*, page 191.

16This is the difference between choosing between separate acts, and choosing between whole ways of life. In this realm none of us can act, without blindness, except by revelation. The Prophet said, "A man can do nothing for himself unless God directs him in the right way and the priesthood is for that purpose." *Ibid.*, page 364.

make all-time binding decisions, eternal covenants.[17] Once made, once "renewed and confirmed," they free us from the life-wasting torment of "bringing it all up" over and over. The decisions, as it were, reverberate through the whole galaxy.[18] And even the lesser roles of life, its distractions and setbacks, take on color and creativity as instruments of the larger "becoming."

Why is it, we may ask, that the Father and the Son "cannot" break their eternal compacts?[19] Because they are "unfree" in attitude? Just the opposite. Because they have made everlasting covenant that they will express freedom in the fullest way, to the resounding blessing of the whole human family.[20] For us, such a decision requires incalculably more intelligent use of individual talent than does shrinking postponement of decision. Made in imitation of the Divine, man's free agency is the boldest, most powerful, most sweeping, and most exciting commitment possible.

Freely we must face it. Out of the eternities we chose and were chosen for light and Divine sonship. Only if we become determined against such a glorious destiny will we avoid the over-arching decisions of direction that bring total freedom. For if we will, our destiny is to become more and more free in the widening circles of fulfillment called Eternal Life.

---

[17]According to the Prophet we already have made such a covenant "before the foundations of the earth were laid." Now, as we mature in the flesh, this "new and everlasting covenant" is "renewed and confirmed" upon us "for the sake of the whole world." Doctrine and Covenants 84:33-40, 48; 86: 8-11.

[18]"The Lord God will disperse the powers of darkness from before you, and cause the heavens to shake for your good, and his name's glory." Ibid., 21:4-6.

[19]This is a "cannot" that reduces to an eternal "will not." It is impossible because He has so chosen, not because external forces prevent it. Another remarkable power of freedom.

[20]"Everlasting covenant was made between three personages before the organization of this earth, and relates to their dispensation of things to men on the earth; these personages, according to Abraham's record, are called God the first, the Creator; God the second, the Redeemer; and God the third, the witness or Testator." Teachings of the Prophet Joseph Smith, page 190.

Revelation and Self-Revelation

There is surely a piece of the Divinity in us.

Something that was before the Elements and owes no homage to the Sun. Nature tells me that I am the Image of God as well as Scripture.

He that understands not this much hath not his introduction or first lesson and is yet to begin the alphabet of man.

— *Sir Thomas Browne, Religio Medici.*

CHAPTER VII

INTENSIVE SELF-ANALYSIS is the preoccupation of our time. Many methods are employed to probe the mysterious regions below the consciousness, regions "sheer, frightful, no-man-fathomed." Out of this has arisen a variety of attempts to define and explain man's religiousness. And thus, for example, there are "reductions" of religion to folk-psychology, or primitive taboo, or flights of wish, or emotional purgation, or aesthetic ritual, etc.

On one point there is surprising agreement among writers otherwise opposed. It is recognition of a wholly unique spread of awareness in man — that is called, by Otto, the "numinous" sense — deep innate sensitivity to something sacred, an underived feeling for the holy, with responses of wonder, awe, and reverence.[1] This, it is claimed by many, is primary, a given fact of human consciousness that cannot be traced to rational or empirical sources. We do not learn it. It is somehow, and strangely, innate.

For this and a vast spectrum of related phenomena, the Prophet Joseph Smith gave a seminal explanation: The heightening sense of light within is rooted in man's spirit. It is not something magically created at birth. It permeates our cumulative heritage of individual awareness and extends infinitely into the past. Its composition is actually derived from a Divine nebula of elements "in which," the Prophet taught, "dwells all the glory."[2]

Explaining the Inexplicable

Attempts to account for the bases of religious consciousness that are "this-worldly," therefore, often leave a great deal un-

---

[1]See Rudolph Otto, *Idea of the Holy*; London, Oxford, Galaxy Paperback. Otto was a German Protestant theologian. Others of varied persuasions who nevertheless agree that the "sacred sense" is the core of religious experience are: Julian Huxley, a Humanist, in *Religion Without Revelation*, New York, Mentor Books, 1964. Rufus Jones, the "mild mystic" of the Society of Friends in *The Radiant Life and A Call to What Is Vital*; New York, Macmillan, 1949. Albert Schweitzer, who has become the living conscience of the 20th Century, in *Out of My Life and Thought*; New York, Mentor, 1960. His code is "reverence for life." Carl Jung, psychoanalyst, speaks of the "collective unconscious" or "symbol-making factory" in man that leads us to religious expression reflecting a kind of "racial memory." *The Undiscovered Self*, New York, Mentor, 1964. Tielhard Chardin, a Catholic scientist, in *The Phenomenon of Man*; New York, Harper Torch book, speaks of a kind of knowledge-sphere which is hidden in us. John Wisdom and Ronald W. Hepburn, both in the positivistic tradition, agree on this sense of holiness. See the latter's *Christianity and Paradox*; London, Watts and Company, 1957. The "depth-theologians," e.g. Tillich, Marcel, and Buber, speak of "intuition" and in various ways hold that "unconditional concern" in man is the foundation of all religion.

[2]*Teachings of the Prophet Joseph Smith*, edited by Joseph Fielding Smith; Deseret News Press, Salt Lake City, Utah, 1958; page 351.

explained or inadequately explained away. But the recognition that religion is more involved in *recovery* than discovery, that our destiny is not union with Divine realities, but *reunion*, opens up a whole new perspective.

Within the framework of Judaeo-Christian assumptions, for example, it aids immensely.

This recognition explains, to begin with, the Prophet's classic statement on religious knowing. Whether written, spoken, or directly presented within, the "word of Jehovah" has such an influence over the human mind, the logical mind, that it is convincing without other testimony.[3] When it comes, he later said, as a flow of pure intelligence attended by a burning in the center self, it is of God.[4] Our search for external warrant is really the confirmation and application of what is already, and more certainly, known.

It aids in comprehending the essence of faith. Faith or trust in the Divine is not a blind leap nor desperate gullibility, not "being crucified on the paradox of the absurd."[5] Faith rests on knowledge and self-knowledge and cannot survive without them. It is the expression of the inner self in harmony with a whole segment of one's prior experiences. These experiences, however hidden under mortal amnesia, are indelible in their effect on our affinities, kinships, and sensitivities.[6]

Understanding our religious destiny clarifies the apparent requirement, which may be said to underlie the whole of the scriptures, that we are expected both to believe and respond. To the query, how can you believe what is utterly unevidenced, the question may be returned, how have you managed to repress the ingrained evidence within? The caution, often justi-

---

[3]*Documentary History of the Church*, Volume V, page 526.

[4]See *Teachings of the Prophet Joseph Smith*, page 151; also Doctrine and Covenants 9:8, 9.

[5]This is one of Kierkegaard's descriptions of the nature of the "leap of faith" to Christ.

[6]Plato's notion of "knowledge by recollection" of a former existence was mainly conceptual or mathematical. For the prophets the awakening of "spirit memories" is also concrete, pictorial, personal. The present world is a grosser duplicate of the heavenly order, whereas Plato's heaven was a realm transcending space, time, and materiality.

fied in religion, that one should not say he knows when he does not know is to be matched with the caution that it is equally deceptive to claim one does not know when, in fact, he does know. Both errors betray and disrupt the self.

This understanding of our relationship to God gives meaning to the theme of modern revelation that the forces of darkness operate by subtraction more than by addition. "That which was from the beginning is plainly manifest unto them," and "every spirit of man was innocent in the beginning." Then "one cometh and *taketh away* light and truth, through disobedience, from the children of men, and because of the tradition of their fathers." (Doctrine and Covenants 93:31, 38, 39.) The love for darkness which follows on the flouting of the inner light often goes under apparently praiseworthy disguises: objectivity, intellectual integrity, precision, strength to resist one's "mere feelings," etc.

This understanding exposes the structure of testimony and the nature of judgment. "Every man whose spirit receiveth not the light is under condemnation. For man is spirit. . . ." (Doctrine and Covenants 93:32, 33.) This is to say, as B. H. Roberts puts it, that the spirit is "native to truth"; that as a flame leaps toward a flame, the soul's very nature is to reach toward and embrace the light. One who thrusts down or represses these sovereign impulses sunders himself. He eventually falls victim, as Jung maintains, to some of the worst forms of psycho-somatic illness and misery. (Contrary to the Freudians, Jung believes one can healthily suppress his more superficial desires, however compulsive, but not these.)[7] Of all the laws of spiritual life, this may be the most fundamental. He who welcomes truth and light, on the other hand, moves toward "a perfect bright recollection" and "receiveth truth and light until he is glorified in truth and knoweth all things," growing "brighter and brighter until the perfect day." (Doctrine and Covenants 93: 28. Compare 50:23, 24; 88:67.)

---

[7]Carl Jung, *Modern Man in Search of a Soul*; New York, Harcourt Brace.

The Uprush and the Downflow

To move from interpretation of the sacred inner life to adequate description is notoriously difficult. Nevertheless, here is an attempt to capture the flavor of the Latter-day Saint "experiment in depth," revelatory touches with the self that seem to disclose the longer-than-mortal sense. (Inevitably we veer into the oblique but somehow more expressive language of simile and metaphor.) There are:

— *Prayer flashes*, when our words outreach thought and we seem to be listening above ourselves, completely at home while we are surprised at hints of hidden spirit memories within.

— *Familiarity of persons*, immediate luminous rapport — this face or that gesture or motion — that elicits the sense of recall, a premortal intimacy, especially in the environs of teaching and being taught.

— *Haunting sensations*, usually visual, sometimes auditory, of a landscape of life or a bitter predicament in the soul, that call up simultaneous feelings of "again" and "for the first time"; like being thrust, as leading actor, into the last act of a play without knowing, and yet almost knowing, what occurred in the first two.

— *Numbing protests* from below sometimes of unrelievable urgency or guilt, that are ruthless in unmasking our pretense. These are not simply the yeas or nays of "conscience" about acts, but bell sounds of a whole self that will not be muffled, that ring with presentiments, thrusting us toward ends that seem tied to an elusive but white-lighted blueprint inside.

— *Shades of consciousness* that occur just at awakening or just before sleep, unpredictably impressing while they express, in images or silent words or free association. By the sanctity of their feeling-tone, these are different than our usual helter-skelter menagerie of thought.

— *Dreams and illusions* that seem not to be mere dreams or mere illusions, catching us quite off-guard and lingering in their after-effect, as if life were a game of internal hide-the-thimble and we were "getting warm" to our own potential.

— *Unaccountable reverberations* (e.g. in tear-filled eye or tingling throat or spine) from a phrase or sentiment (which, for the speaker or writer may be merely parenthetical), or from a strain of music, or some trivial stimulus in the midst of drudgery, bearing a holy atmosphere of spontaneous and total recognition.

— *Reflections of our faces* in the mirror when we look in and not just at, our eyes. As if light were coming to the surface, and a curious recovery, and even awe, of the self occurs. There lurks an autobiography, a soul-story that is foreign, yet intimate, unfolding a more-than-I-thought-I-was.

— *Right-track feelings,* the sense of the foreordained, like emerging from a fever to find that roughshod or happenstance trials have been presided over by some uncanny instinctual self who knows what he is about. Just before or just after turning a crucial corner, this someone nearer than you, that *is* you, holds a quiet celebration that injects peace into the marrow of the bones.

Such flashes and drives are tied to the whole gamut of complex mental life and may have neat and utterly mundane naturalistic explanations (such as the chemistry of the occipital lobe). Yet the joy that comes from these uprisings, rooted, as they seem to be, in some more primal creative being and that, in turn, in God, supersedes any of the pleasures of human possession or external manipulation.

Cleaning the Lampshade

Much of modern life is a darkening process, cutting us off from the uprush of the fountain at our center. The lives we live and the demands of environment to which science and technology and strategy are admirably adapted, tend to lead us toward self-estrangement.

Becoming more out of alignment with our inner selves, straining to present faces that are acceptable to the world, we suffer a shallowing effect. And what William James called "the Energies of Men" are trapped and suffocated, because we are afraid of being deluded, we have a revulsion at many forms of religion, and a kind of psychological hypochondria which makes us suspect our subconscious is solely inhabited by snakes and spiders.

Was it a sort of ancient hoodwink the Master recommended — these strange sentences about "becoming as a little child"? Are the virtues of the childlike more obvious than the vices of the childish?

Maybe He was saying more, saying that we are not, as empiricists assert, born an empty tablet on which the chalk of childhood writes. Maybe He was saying that a child has swift, untinctured affinity and response to his own burning deeps. He is exemplary not, as is so often said, in vulnerable readiness to believe others' voices, but in soul-unity that prevents disbelief of his own. He has a whole, happy, healthy relationship with the core of creativity and spirituality which is his glory-laden spirit.

If so, the explicit and expansive messages of Messiah, "bringing all things to their remembrance," would shine more clearly through the boy Samuel, the boy Nephi, or the boy Joseph, and likewise the childlike Adam who, though he was centuries old when the human race was in its infancy, vibrated with prophetic vision. That would explain the verse, added by the Prophet, to the biblical account of the youth of Christ Himself: "He needed not that any man should teach Him."[8] God, to reveal Himself to Christ, needed only to reveal Christ to Himself, in "the glory he had with Him before the foundations of the world." Is it really different with us?[9]

---

[8]See the Prophet's inspired version of Matthew 3 (he adds three verses). "And it came to pass that Jesus grew up with his brethren, and waxed strong, and waited upon the Lord for the time of his ministry to come. And he served his father, and he spake not as other men, neither could he be taught; for he needed not that any man should teach him. And after many years, the hour of his ministry drew nigh." (Matthew 3:24-26.)

[9]In his greatest discourse the Prophet testified of the interdependence of knowledge of God and knowledge of self. "If men do not comprehend the character of God, they do not comprehend themselves." *Teachings of the Prophet Joseph Smith*, page 343.

Index

A

Adam, 77
Added upon, those who are, 32
Adler, Alfred, 36
Affinities, 73
Affliction, good may arise from, 59
Age, 26
Amnesia, 20
Analysis, existential, 65
Angels, 37
Anguish, the price of, 50-51
Annihilation, 48
Anxiety toward the future, 65
Anthropomorphism, 35-36, 39
Aquinas, Thomas, 14, 16
Assumptions, Judaeo-Christian, 73
Attitude toward life, the humanist, 31
Augustine, 14, 28
Autonomy, 25

B

Barth, 38
Becoming, 69
Behaviorists, 18
Being, modes of, 17
Beginning, in the, 65-66
Berdyaev, 16, 65
Bergson, Henri, 18
Birth, 14
  the second, 40
Blame, the chain of, 68
Blasphemy, 39
Bodies, advantages of having, 43
Body, the 17, 30
  and the spirit, 43-51
  impairment by, 47-48
  man not imprisoned in, 51
  sole source of happiness, 41
  the living temple of Spirit of God, 50
  the product of righteousness, 48
  what is good and evil of, 48-50
Boehme, Jacob, 47
Brightman, Edgar Sheffield, 19
Buber, Martin, 38
Buddha, 48

C

Capacities, 17, 18
Chance, 65
Character, addictions of, 68
Child, becoming as a, 77
Christendom, orthodox, 27-28, 31
Commitment, necessary for freedom, 69-70
Compacts, eternal, 70
Confusion, intellectual, 38
Conscience, 75
Consciousness, 25, 29, 30
  levels of, 47
  shades of, 75
"Cosmic dust," 30
Covenants, eternal, 69
Creation, absolute mysterious act of God, 28
  God's continual, 27
  never totally original, 26
  of spirit or soul, 14
  paradoxes of, 14, 16
  shifting of molecules, 30
  the soul's, 19
"Creation and Procreation," 33-42
Creativity, the core of, 77

D

Death, 26
Decisions, 66
  all-time binding, 69

D

Deity, 35
Descartes, 17
Destiny, conditioning of man's, 35
  man's, 66
  reunion with Divine realities, 73
  understanding our religious, 73
Determinism, 64
Development, capacity for, 25
Devil, the, 68
Dionysius, 35
Disillusion of our time, 68
Divine, manlike qualities not to be applied to, 35
Doctrine, New Dispensation, 31
Downflow, the, 75-76
Dreams, 75
Dualism, between Divine and human, 37
Dualisms, 44

E

Eddinton, Arthur S., 64
Element, 14
  uncreated, 18
Elements, ordering of, 16
Emotions, grosser, 41
Energies of men, 76
Ennoblement, through suffering, 59
Entity, a material, 17
Environment, everlasting, 66
Eternal Life, 70
Eternalism, concept of personal, 24
Eternity, 26, 34
  a temporal, 46
Evil, problem of, 15, 18-19
"Evil and Suffering," 53-61
Existence, conscious and purposive, 15
  fundamental, 16
Existentialism, 28-29, 31
Existenz-philosophy, 15
Extinction, utter, 15

F

Faces, reflections of, 76
Faith, rests on knowledge and self-knowledge, 73
"Familiar and Familial, The," 34-37
Familiarity of persons, 75
Family, blessing of the human, 70
  organization of the human, 21
Fatalists, 18
Fatherhood, Divine and human, 34-37
  not to be applied to God, 35-36
Feelings, finer, 41
  right-track, 76
Feuerbach, L., 36
"First Cause," 65
Foreknowledge, 68
Foundations, shaking of the, 25
Free Agency, most powerful commitment, 70
Freedom, 30
  foreshortened or denied, 28
  problem of human, 15, 17-18
"Freedom and Fulfillment," 63-70
Freedoms, the four, 67
Freud, 22

G

Ghandi, 46
Glory, fullness of, 48
God, 34, 65, 73, 77
  based on "contingency," 16
  doctrine of transcendent, 38-39
  eternal compact made by, 70
  father of spirit of man, 37
  his love for man, 41
  man may be fashioned like unto, 51
  objection to belief in a personal, 51

78

operates within eternal limits, 19
  some in terror of, 56
  the Father, 18
  transmitting of spirit traits by, 37
  understanding our relationship to, 74
God of the Creeds, 56
Godliness, 40
  power of, 41
Gods, the making of, 18
Gospel plan, the, 18
Gratitude, 41
Guilt, 39
  toward the past, 65

H

Handicaps, 58
Happiness, 41
  great principle of, 43
Heaven, first organization in, 21
Heidegger, 22, 65
Heraclitus, 14
"Holy of Holies," 20
Hopes, subjective, 36
Humanism, 30-31, 32
Hume, 14, 15

I

Identity, 26
  problem of, 14, 15-16
  ultimate, 23
"Identity or Nothing," 23-32
Idolatry, 39
Illness, psychic, 21
Illusions, 55, 75
Immaterialism, 44, 45, 50
Immaterialists, 46, 47, 48
Immortality, inevitable and universal, 26
Imprisonment, perpetuated, 68
Indeterminism, 64
Individuality, 24
Inequalities, 18
Inequality, human, 53
Inexplicable, explaining the, 72-74
Initiative, intelligent, 69
Inspiration, 40
Intellect, disparagements of, 17
Intelligence, 17
  elements composing, 15
  of spirits, 14
  possibilities of prime, 66
  primal, 18, 23
  uncreated, 66
  unoriginated and indestructible, 25
Intelligences, 26
  characteristics of, 24-25
Introspection, inspired, 20
Irreverence, 38-39

J

James, William, 20, 76
Jehovah, the word of, 73
Jesus Christ, 18, 21, 34, 49, 57
  came to end needless suffering, 58, 59
  did not need teachers, 77
  purpose of His life and death, 51
  second birth through, 40
  the Master Teacher, 20
  to break bonds of diminishing freedom, 69
Job, 15
Jones, Rufus, 20
Joy, everlasting, 18
  fullness of, 48, 49
  in the image of Christ, 61
Judgment, nature of, 74
Jung, Carl B., 15, 21, 74

K

Kierkegaard, 16, 29
Kingdom, celestial, 43
Kinships, 73
Knowledge, 73

L

Law, the guarantor of freedom, 67
Laws, of spiritual life, 74
Leibnitz, G. W., 15
Liberty, 67
Liberty Jail, 67
Life, interpretation of sacred, inner, 75
  laws of spiritual, 74
  modern, 76
  "the sickness unto death," 29
Light, 74
Love, 38-41
  the essence of, 59

M

Maimonides, 35
Malajustment, religious, 21
Man, a phantom, 28
  a temporary event, 30
  acts of, 27
  awareness in, 72
  chosen for Divine sonship, 70
  creation of, 27
  derivation of, 13
  freedom and enlargement of, 27
  individuality and consciousness of, 28
  may be fashioned like unto God, 51
  Father of spirit of, 37
  Godlike qualities not to be applied to, 35
  godliness engrained in, 40
  his destiny, 66
  his ills began with body, 48
  eternal intelligence of, 34
  is eternal, 23
  never totally a product, 65
  the viper within, 21
  threefold nature of, 47
  ultimate identity of, 23
Marcel, Gabriel, 16, 29, 38, 50
Mary, mother of Christ, 36-37
Matter, 30
Mechanists, 18
Memory, 26
Men, energies of, 76
Menninger, 50
Meno, The, 15
Milton, John, 36
Mind, the, 26, 30
Mind-body problem, 17
Minds, susceptible of enlargement, 25
Misery, human, 54
Mission in this world, 58
Moments, sacred, 20
Montague, William Peperell, 30
Mortality, 19, 20
  might have been avoided, 19
Motivation to share, 41
Mystery, the retreat to, 54
Mystics, 46

N

Nature, 65
Needs, individual, 58
Negation, anguish of absolute, 29
Nephi, 77
Niebuhr, 22, 38
Nietzsche, 47, 65
Nihilism, 29
Nihilists, 19
Nothingness of nothing, the, 31

O

"O My Father," 42
Organisms, one-celled, 30
Originator, an, 16
Origins, seek thine, 23
Otto, Rudolph, 20, 72

P

Pain, a laboratory of soul-nurture, 60
Paradox, conquest of, 37-38
Pascal, 28
Peace of soul, 41
Perfection, 58
Personality, 38-39
   celestial, 51
Persons, familiarity of, 75
Pessimism, 29
Physicalism, 45, 50
Physicalists, 46, 47
Plato, 15
Potential, killing our own, 67
Power of love, 41
Praise, 69
Prayer, 49, 75
Predestinationists, 18
Pre-existence, 14, 18
   awareness of, 22
Preface, viii
Pride, slavery to, 67
Problem, mind-body, 17
Procreation, Divine, 14
Prophets, revelations of the, 21
Protests, numbing, 75
Psychoanalysis, 15
Psychologism, 36-37, 39
Psychiatrist, the Perfect, 22
Purification, processes of, 49

Q

Quantity of selves, fixed, 26

R

Realities, pre-causation of, 16
Reality, 55
Recollection, 20
Reflections, patterns of ordinary, 15
Regeneration, 49
Regression, permanent, 15
Rejoicing, experience of, 50
Relationship to God, understanding our, 74
Religion, involved in recovery, 73
   reductions of, 72
Religiousness, man's, 71
Responsibility, brother to freedom, 68
Resurrection, losses to be made up in, 61
Revelation, flashes of, 61
"Revelation and Self-Revelation," 71-77
Reverence or irreverence, 38-39
Reverberations, unaccountable, 76
Rewording, rewarding, 26
Righteousness, the product of, 48
Roberts, B. H., 74
Russell, Bertrand, 15, 30
Ryle, Gilbert, 17

S

St. John of the Cross, 46
Samuel, 77
Sanctification, way of, 49
Sanity, the superiority of, 50
Sartre, 16, 65
Satan, 57
Self-analysis, 71-72
Self-awareness, 15
   problem of, 19-22

Self-elements, interaction of, 17
Self-estrangement, 76
Selfhood, 15
   the elements of, 45
Self-knowledge, 73
Self-made, 69
Self-unity, 50
Selves, quantity of, 26
Sensations, haunting, 75
Sense, the "numinous," 72
Sensitivities, 73
Smith, Joseph, 13, 45, 67
   his vision, 34
   on truth, 22
   on ultimate identity of man, 23, 31-32
   teachings on man, 47
Snow, Eliza R., 42
Socrates, 20, 41, 47
Soul, creation of, 14
   to cultivate the, 47
Soul-sickness, 68
Spirit, 17
   creation of the, 14
   Divinely sired, 23
   Father of, 37
   man's, 35, 77
   native to truth, 74
   the immortal, 33
"Spirit and the Body, The," 43-51
Spirit-personality, 46
Spirits, embodied and disembodied, 46
   intelligence of, 14
   procreated by God, 34
   susceptible of enlargement, 25
Spirituality, core of, 77
Stoic, a kind of, 31
Suffering, in vain, 61
   needless, 58, 59
   problem of, 18-19
Suicide, 26, 29
Sympathy, 41

T

Tabernacle Choir, Mormon, 42
Teacher, religious, 20
Teachings of the Prophet Joseph Smith,
   21, 22, 23, 24, 27, 33, 35, 60
Testimony, 74
Theologians, Western, 18
"Things More Noble," 39-48
Tillich, Paul, 29, 38
Trail, the luminous, 20
"Transcendent, the," 38
Tribulations, 60
Trinity, the immaterial, 37
Truth, 22, 74
   the redeeming, 51

U

Universe, the, 18
Uprush, the, 75-76

V

Virtue, 41
   intellectual confusion a religious, 38
Von Braun, Wernher, 30

W

"Whence Cometh Man," 13-22
Wholeness, joy that accompanies, 49
   restoration of, 50
Wisdom, John, 18, 19
Woman, derivation of, 13
Wordsworth, William, 20
World, material, 17
Worlds, spiritual and heavenly, 14